# TITO'S SEPARATE ROAD

America and Yugoslavia in World Politics

# TITO'S SEPARATE ROAD

America and Yugoslavia
in World Politics

*by* JOHN C. CAMPBELL

*Published for the*
Council on Foreign Relations
by
Harper & Row, Publishers
*New York and Evanston*

The Council on Foreign Relations is a nonprofit institution devoted to the study of political, economic, and strategic problems as related to American foreign policy. It takes no stand, expressed or implied, on American policy.

The authors of books published under the auspices of the Council are responsible for their statements of fact and expressions of opinion. The Council is responsible only for determining that they should be presented to the public.

For a list of Council publications see pages 177-180.

TITO'S SEPARATE ROAD
AMERICA AND YUGOSLAVIA IN WORLD POLITICS

Copyright © 1967 by Council on Foreign Relations, Inc.
*All rights reserved, including the right to reproduce
this book or any portion thereof in any form.
For information, address Harper & Row, Publishers, Incorporated
49 East 33rd Street, New York, N.Y. 10016*

FIRST EDITION

*Library of Congress catalog card number: 67-15967*
*Printed in the United States of America*
*Published by Harper & Row, Publishers, Incorporated*

D-R

To Mary Hillis Campbell
with thanks for her
interest and her tolerance.

## IN MEMORY OF EDWARD JOHN NOBLE

The Policy Book series of the Council on Foreign Relations is published under a grant from the Edward John Noble Foundation in memory of Mr. Noble and his interest in encouraging American leadership.

# Policy Books of the Council on Foreign Relations

The Council on Foreign Relations undertook its Policy Book series with the idea of presenting timely analysis and recommendations on subjects of current import in world affairs. These books are not the product of exhaustive research or of lengthy discussion by study groups. Each is in the nature of an extended essay by an individual author who has had long or particularly intensive acquaintance with his chosen subject. The intention is to contribute to constructive thinking on American policies, present and future.

The subject of American policy toward Yugoslavia goes far beyond the pattern of bilateral relations with a single country; it has involved, simultaneously, issues connected with policy toward the Soviet Union, Eastern Europe, China, the third world, and the Western community. It throws light on such broad questions as the future of Communist societies and the promise and limits of "peaceful coexistence" in Europe. The very complexities of Yugoslavia's role in world affairs, plus the American propensity to very simple approaches to it, have contributed to a lack of understanding in this country on how it affects our own immediate and long-term interests. Thus, while a series of American administrations of both major parties since 1948 produced a remarkable continuity of policy, it has been anything but easy to carry out. This book assesses those difficulties, reviews past policies, and looks to the future.

The Policy Books are deliberately kept brief, not with the aim of simplification but to present with a minimum of factual background and detail the reasoned conclusions of individual authors with special experience and qualifications. This volume runs slightly longer than the average, partly because of the editor's lack of success in persuading the author to cut it down.

The views and conclusions are those of the author, not of the Council on Foreign Relations, its staff, or any study group. The Council takes responsibility for the decision to publish it as a contribution to thought on a subject which has been close to the center of world politics ever since Tito astonished the world by his defiance of Stalin in 1948.

JOHN C. CAMPBELL
Editor

ACKNOWLEDGMENT

I should like to express my thanks to the many officers of the Department of State and the American Foreign Service, of the Yugoslav government, and of other governments, with whom I have discussed Yugoslav affairs. Their contributions to my own thinking, if they could be identified, would have to remain anonymous in any case but are none the less gratefully acknowledged.

Some of the matters dealt with in this book were the subject of discussion by a small study group which met at the Council several years ago under the chairmanship of Frank Altschul. I derived much profit from those meetings. In addition, several individuals read all or parts of the manuscript and commented critically on it. I am particularly grateful to R. V. Burks, Stephen D. Kertesz, and Richard Rowson for their extensive commentary.

Hamilton Fish Armstrong, Editor of *Foreign Affairs,* has had a long-standing interest in Yugoslav matters and a knowledge of them far deeper than my own. His comments have been much appreciated. I am indebted also to George S. Franklin, Jr., and to David W. MacEachron for their suggestions; to Donald Wasson and Janet Rigney of the Council's Library; to Robert W. Valkenier for editorial assistance; and especially to Helen Caruso, whose combined contribution of research support and typing and retyping of the chapters was indispensable.

J.C.C.

# Contents

# TITO'S SEPARATE ROAD

America and Yugoslavia in World Politics

*Chapter I*

# Introduction

Yugoslavia is a small and far from wealthy Balkan country of some 20 million people. Before the Second World War its role was much like that of any other country of central and southeastern Europe. Like them, it was absorbed in territorial disputes with its neighbors. Like them, it was subjected to a variety of pressures and blandishments on the part of rival European powers interested in maintaining or shifting the balance of power against each other. More than most, it was torn by internal stress and threatened in its very existence by the struggle of nationalities within its own borders. It had no pretensions to an important part in world politics and no real possibilities of playing such a part.

In late 1944 Yugoslavia emerged from military defeat, partition, enemy occupation, and a fierce partisan struggle that was also a civil war, under a Communist regime led by Josip Broz-Tito. In its first few years that regime was in close alliance with the Soviet Union. It acted as a militant vanguard of Communist expansion into Central and Southern Europe, exerting pressure on Austria, Italy, and Greece. On two occasions, in 1945 at Trieste and 1946 when two American planes were shot down in Yugoslavia, it came to the verge of open conflict with the United States.

In 1948 that same regime shattered the unity of the Communist bloc by defying Stalin. About a year later it was moving into a relationship of extensive, though by no means unreserved, practical cooperation with the West. At the same time it gloried in the role of independent Marxist state, inviting those Communist states still subject to Soviet control to follow its example and seeking ties with the newly established Communist regime in China. In the mid-1950s it staked out for itself a position as a leader of the nonaligned states, a group growing in numbers every year with the progressive breakup of the European colonial empires.

Yugoslavia's relations with the Soviet Union, after Stalin's death, went through an alternating pattern of reconciliation and bitter discord that must have bewildered the men in the Kremlin as much as the leaders of the West. Even before the outbreak of the Soviet-Chinese dispute, Yugoslavia found itself the target of Peking's most scathing denunciations of "revisionism" and treason to the Communist cause, a development which in time drew it ever closer to Moscow. But it never yielded a whit of its independence. The Tito regime continued to proclaim its devotion to the "international workers' movement," but without recognizing the primacy of any Communist state or party and at the same time assuring the West of its desire for normal relations and mutual cooperation. Through all these vagaries it never ceased to interest itself, and to try to exert its influence, in every critical situation from Cuba to the Congo to Vietnam. And always its representatives spoke with a loud voice in the United Nations.

It may be said, justly, that the Yugoslav leaders have attempted a role in world politics far beyond the capacity of the resources of the country to sustain. The fact remains that they have propelled Yugoslavia into the center of the main issues of our time: the struggle between the Soviet Union and the West, the changing relationships among Communist states and parties, the ideological and other questions in dispute between Moscow and Peking, the relations of the underdeveloped with the developed and of the uncommitted with the committed, arms control and disarmament, and the future of Europe, to say nothing of a host of lesser matters of concern to the chancelleries of the world.

That the policies of Yugoslavia have been important to the

United States may be inferred from the attention which Washington has given to them: the time and deliberation which have gone into weighing and defining American policies toward that country and the resources which have gone into carrying them out. It can be and has been argued that some or all of these American policies have been ill conceived or fruitless. The subject has raised a good deal of domestic controversy since 1948 and continues to do so, without ever having been subjected to a searching and reasoned public debate.

In the view of the United States government, especially of its Executive Branch, Yugoslavia's position and policies have remained over the years of great significance in the wider questions of Western relations with the Soviet Union, with other Communist countries, and with the rest of the world. American aid to Yugoslavia, however the balance of motives behind it shifted as conditions changed, was begun under President Truman and continued by administrations of both parties because of their shared conviction that what Yugoslavia stood for, and the main thrust of the policies it was following, directly or indirectly served the interests and objectives of the United States and of the free world. Aid has tapered off in recent years. Its urgency has obviously decreased in the eyes both of Belgrade and of Washington. The fundamental question is whether the main elements of the policy of which aid was an instrument remain valid.

It is necessary to examine the considerations on which American policies toward Yugoslavia have been based in the past and to reach some conclusion on the relative success or inadequacy of those policies. That is the burden of the chapters immediately following. But this book is not intended primarily as a review or critique of the record of the past. Its principal inquiry is directed to the problems of today and of tomorrow, to Yugoslavia's situation now, to its policies foreign and domestic, and to the choices before the United States in determining its course in relation to that country. Have we given it too much attention? Has Yugoslavia lost much of its significance in international politics now that it has made its peace with Moscow without giving up its independence, and now that the Soviet empire from which it broke away no longer exists in anything like its old form? Some informed observers believe this to be the case. It is the argument of this book that, while many things have changed, including the nature of the "Communist world," the course taken by Yugoslavia continues to be directly relevant to the vital questions at issue among Communist states and between those states and the West.

\* \* \*

There is a danger in looking at any state merely as the concrete expression of a doctrine or ideology, whether it be Communist or some other; and if Communist, whether it be "revisionist" or "dogmatist." It may be more important that a state bears a Russian, Chinese, or Yugoslav stamp. Especially with Yugoslavia it is necessary always to come back to the people, to their land and their history, and to the relationships of individuals and of nationalities which are the stuff of Yugoslav politics. The future of Yugoslavia is doubtless heavily dependent on what happens within the League of Communists, now the ruling party. The future of communism in that country, on the other hand, has been and will be shaped primarily by the Yugoslav environment. Thus it is necessary, first of all, to state a few elementary facts about Yugoslavia.

A South Slav, asked what is his ethnic nationality, will identify himself as a Serb, a Croat, a Slovene, or a Macedonian, or possibly as a Montenegrin or a Bosnian Moslem. The non-Slavic inhabitant of the country will call himself a member of his minority nationality—Hungarian, Albanian, Rumanian, or whatever. It is a rarity to find a self-proclaimed Yugoslav. A generation ago King Alexander used to say he was the only Yugoslav in the country. Today it is Tito himself who perhaps comes nearest to fitting that description: a man born in the border area between Croatia and Slovenia, a participant in the Russian civil war, for years a worker in a movement in which loyalty was to class and to communism and to Stalin rather than to nation, a leader in resistance to Hitler and then to Stalin in the name of Serbs and Croats and Slovenes alike, and finally president of the whole country standing above its separate nationalities.

The ruling party, however, has been anything but immune to

the currents of national sentiment and identification that dominate popular attitudes. Every Yugoslav citizen knows that this leading member of the party is a Serb, that one a Croat, and the other a Slovene. Yugoslavia is a federal state, its constituent republics based on historic units generally following the lines of ethnic individuality: Serbia, Croatia, Slovenia, Bosnia-Herzegovina (which is mixed Serb, Croat, and Moslem), Montenegro (which is Serb, but Serb of the special Montenegrin kind), and Macedonia (now nurtured as a separate nationality largely to negate claims from across the border that the people are really Bulgarian). Some republics are separated from others by language, some by religion; some contain mixtures of both; each has its own traditions. Practically every political or economic decision of any importance, taken at the federal or at the republic level, has its reflections in the way people think about it, or act on it, as members of their respective nationalities.

Why, then, does Yugoslavia exist at all? Some extreme Serbian or Croatian nationalists say it is held together only by the iron Communist dictatorship, which denies the right of self-determination. It is nearer to the truth to say that a single Yugoslav state, doubtful as its stability may be, exists because each of its national groups would face a more dubious future outside. The first united Yugoslav state, built from independent Serbia and from pieces of the collapsing Ottoman and Hapsburg empires in the second decade of this century, was nearly torn apart by the fierce struggle of Catholic Croat against Orthodox Serb and finally came to grief in the Second World War amidst foreign invasion, civil strife, and unspeakable massacres. It was to the credit of the partisan movement, even though the main motive of its Communist leaders was to gain political power, that it preached reconciliation among the nationalities and the need for a new order based on equality and mutual understanding. It was a message of hope to Yugoslavia's peoples as they struggled desperately against Hitler's forces of invasion and occupation, and a way out of the fatal consequences of nationalism carried to extremes of mass slaughter.

The Communist party, while it indulged in many violent and ruthless actions against individuals and groups during the period of building its power, deserves credit for holding the lid on explosive forces that might have reduced the country to chaos. But two decades of Communist rule have not eliminated dislike and jealously and conflict among Yugoslavia's nationalities. They have taken new forms. They have penetrated into the party itself. The great questions affecting Yugoslavia's future are, internally, the nature of the political and economic system that is developing, and externally, relations with Russia and with the West. In both, the relations among Yugoslavia's own nationalities will bear significantly, perhaps decisively, on the outcome.

\*     \*     \*

One other basic factor which goes deeper than current regimes and doctrines should be mentioned here, because it tends to be lost from view when governments fix their eyes on the specific elements of short-term national interest or limit their horizons within the familiar confines of their own accepted ideologies. That is the inclination of the South Slav peoples to look westward as well as eastward for cultural and political ties. Croatia and Slovenia were for centuries parts of the Austrian Empire; although they eventually broke away from Vienna and Budapest, their whole culture was and remained Western and Catholic. South of the Sava and the Danube lived the Serbs, first under Turkish domination for five hundred years and then independent. From the time of their national awakening, which began about two centuries ago, they looked for sympathy and support alternately to Mother Russia, to which they felt linked by religion and a common Slavic origin, and to the West.

It was Western cultural influence, German ideas of national culture and French ideas of democracy, which had the greater role in inspiring the national movements and in creating the intellectual and popular basis for a united South Slav state. In the First World War it was Western Allied troops under French command who helped to rescue the Serbs from their terrible ordeal under German occupation. It was the United States which proclaimed the Fourteen Points with their stress on self-determination for Europe's peoples. Woodrow Wilson did his utmost at the Peace Conference to prevent the cession of large parts of ethnically Yugoslav territory to Italy. Between the two world wars, Yugloslavia was a participant in the French system of alliances, and popular sympathies remained with the Western democracies when the government chose to compromise with Hitler's Germany. Another factor which added a special dimension to Yugoslav-American relations, though it had no direct influence on policy, were the ties between the hundreds of thousands of Yugoslav immigrants to the United States and the lands of their origin.

These traditions and sentiments were not wiped out, when Yugoslavia came under Communist rule, merely by being designated as "bourgeois." The Yugoslav people were aware that their resistance to the Germans during the Second World War had received far more help from the Western powers than from the Soviet Union, and that the relief and rehabilitation supplies poured into the country by UNRRA after the war all came from the West.

One cannot say how much popular support the Tito regime had when it came to power, for it did not choose to submit to the test of a free election. Some areas and some social groups were favorable; but neither in Serbia, where the partisan movement made little headway during the war, nor in Croatia was the enthusiasm as marked as the suspicion and hostility. The Communist party established a monopoly of political power and has held it ever since. Nevertheless, it can be said with some assurance that never has the regime had so much popular support as when it broke with the Soviet Union, began to seek new ways at home, and opened the doors to cooperation with the West. And since that time it has not been justified to speak of the sharp line of separation between regime and people that existed in the earlier years. The total and loyal support of "the working people" to which the official pronouncements refer is more propaganda than reality, yet it is equally oversimplified and equally distorted to see everything that happens in Yugoslavia as part of a continuing struggle between the people and the dictatorship.

Yugoslavia's Communist leadership has now been in power for more than twenty years. It is accepted by the people, happily or grudgingly as the individual case may be, because there is no political alternative, but also because they have seen that the system, as it evolves, can maintain the country's independence, provide them with a freer and better life, and keep open the channels of communication and contact with the outside world.

The Yugoslav Communist party (now called League of Communists), moreover, has not been a mere creature of a foreign government or international apparatus, totally outside the mainstream of the life of the nation. In the national election of 1920 the Communists won 58 out of 419 seats in the legislature, after which their party was outlawed. In the 1930s, although the party was torn by dissension and under Stalin's wing, it still attracted a considerable proportion of the most talented and capable young men and women, especially among the university students. And in the wartime resistance against the Germans, the partisan movement included thousands of fighters representing all of Yugoslavia's nationalities who, whether in desperation or in hope, followed Communist leadership. It is true that the Communist leaders at that time were preaching freedom and democracy. But even when they ignored both and established a one-party dictatorship, the party which they led was not like those which the Soviet Union put in power in neighboring Hungary or Rumania. Yugoslavia's Communist party came to power through an indigenous revolution. It had roots in Yugoslav soil. It had, therefore, some sensitivity to popular wishes, although that was scarcely apparent in the early period of pitiless suppression of political opponents, nationalists and democrats as well as fascists and collaborators. And it had within its ranks many to whom the national struggle of the war years was more important than any ideology, especially one of foreign provenance.

The ruling group has to take those considerations into account, especially when the ice on which it is skating, both in domestic and foreign policy, is thin. The United States and other Western nations must take them into account also, if their policies are to rest on anything more firm than day-to-day relations with a group whose actions in the future, as in the past, may be unpredictable and at times hostile. This is the old question the United States has faced many times and in many parts of the world: how to carry on policies toward a people without endorsing or fully supporting their existing government, especially when it is not representative or responsive to their wishes. It is a question which has no standard answer, if it has an answer at all. Each individual case has its own angles. All that is suggested here is that the United States should remain aware of the peoples of Yugoslavia and of elements which lie under the surface of official policies and statements. One of those elements is a strong tradition of friendship for the West.

All these peculiarities of the history and politics of the South Slav peoples have their relevance for any outside power, such as the United States, attempting to work out a satisfactory policy over the years. The United States first began to develop a "Yugoslav policy" in 1948 as a direct response to one simple question: Should a dissident Communist regime be supported against Moscow? The story of American policy since that time has revolved round the continuing validity of its positive answer to that proposition as circumstances have changed and as the complex patterns of Yugoslav and Communist politics have created situations in which neither the questions nor the answers are so simple or so clear.

## Chapter II

# 1948: The Break

In 1945, Edvard Kardelj, Tito's right-hand man, is reported to have said that Soviet-Yugoslav relations should be based on the prospect of Yugoslavia's incorporation as a constituent republic in the Soviet Union.[1] In 1948, that same Kardelj signed with Tito a letter to Stalin and Molotov in which they said that "no matter how much each of us loves the land of Socialism, the Soviet Union, he can in no case love less his country, which is also building Socialism."[2] The first statement, although uttered in connection with ill feeling over the question of Trieste, was linked with a request for "advice which would direct the internal and foreign policy of Yugoslavia along the right path." It reflected a gross misunderstanding of the Stalinist system, with which by definition no Yugoslav Communist could see the possibility of basic conflict. The second statement was the reflection of three years of bitter experience.

That intervening period, which still has many obscurities, was critical for the future of the Communist world. At the time, Western governments and experts were ignorant of much that

[1] Statement made to Soviet Ambassador Sadchikov, June 5, 1945, quoted in the letter of the Central Committee of the Soviet Communist party to the Central Committee of the Communist party of Yugoslavia, May 4, 1948, published in *The Soviet-Yugoslav Dispute* (London: Royal Institute of International Affairs, 1948), p. 38. The Yugoslav government has not confirmed Kardelj's statement, for which the Soviet government remains the only source.

[2] *The Soviet-Yugoslav Dispute*, p. 19.

was happening in Yugoslav-Soviet relations. They saw Yugoslavia as the most enthusiastic and loyal satellite, carrying out Soviet desires in provocative policies toward the West, in feeding the fires of the Greek civil war, and in badgering Italy on the Trieste question. What we did not know—though we might have had some inkling of it had we been sharp enough to see bits of evidence that were plain enough in retrospect when the dispute broke out into the open—was that the Kremlin had quarreled with Tito even during the war and that he had deliberately ignored Soviet advice; that he resented Stalin's deal with the West on Yugoslavia at Yalta; that he had pushed harder to get Trieste than the Russians were prepared to go and had rebuked them in a public speech in 1945 which warned outside powers against treating lightly Yugoslavia's vital interests; that there was no common strategy for supporting the Communist rebellion in Greece or for dealing with the "government" of the rebel leader, Markos; that the Soviet Union took Bulgaria's side in opposing a Yugoslav plan to bring Bulgaria into the Yugoslav federal union as its seventh republic; that Yugoslavia's postwar five-year plan, far from being made in Moscow, was regarded in Moscow as unwise and in some respects absurd; or that the Yugoslavs, through their negotiations with the Soviet Union on joint companies for air and river navigation, were incensed over the obvious desire of the larger partner to exploit the smaller.

Much of this information came out after 1948, although Yugoslav officials, even after establishing easy and rather cordial relations with Westerners, always retained a certain reserve when it came to discussing their relations with the Russians in that earlier period. Part of the story appeared in the documents published by the disputants at the time of the break. Other revelations, such as Moša Pijade's account of the wartime differences and Vladimir Dedijer's biography of Tito, were put out for the edification of world opinion with the blessing of the Yugoslav government.[3] It remained for Milovan Djilas, with the blessing of no one except his American publisher, to show by recounting

---

[3] Moša Pijade, *La fable de l'aide soviétique à l'insurrection nationale yougoslave* (Paris: Livre Yougoslave, 1950); Vladimir Dedijer, *Tito* (New York: Simon and Shuster, 1953).

his personal experience the process of disillusionment of the Yugoslav leaders as they came to know what Stalin and Soviet methods were really like.[4]

## June 28, 1948

June 28 was the date on which Stalin, through a resolution of the Communist Information Bureau endorsed by its nine Communist parties (other than the Yugoslav party), read the "Tito clique" out of the Soviet camp and the world Communist movement. Probably by accident, the Soviet leader chose a fatal day in South Slav history, adding a symbolic meaning to the event in Yugoslav eyes. For June 28 is *Vidov Dan*, St. Vitus' Day, celebrated by Serbs as a day of national mourning and dedication ever since the Turkish armies extinguished Serbian independence on the Field of the Blackbirds in Kossovo in 1389. It was on June 28, also, that a Yugoslav youth named Gavrilo Princip in 1914 fired the shots that killed Archduke Franz Ferdinand, leading to a world war and eventually to the creation of a united South Slav state.

These events of the past were not irrelevant in 1948, for the dispute was not primarily about the fine points of Marxist theory and practice which studded the accusations of the Cominform resolution and the replies of the Yugoslav Communist party. Tito and his colleagues were charged with departing from the correct Marxist path, establishing a bureaucratic regime, slighting the role of the party and dissolving it in the mass "front" organization, misunderstanding the relationship of proletariat and peasantry, adopting "adventurous" policies, and—an insult calculated to infuriate the Yugoslavs—using "purely Turkish terrorist" methods. Some of their policies were pictured as repeating the mistakes of the Mensheviks, others, as similar to those advocated by Trotsky in his day. But the heart of the dispute concerned something else. It concerned who was to control Yugoslavia, Stalin or Tito. As in the past, it was a question of Yugoslavs standing up to a great power and asserting the right to independence. In its origins this was a conflict between Commu-

4 Milovan Djilas, *Conversations with Stalin* (New York: Harcourt, Brace & World, 1962).

nists, and between parties rather than nations. But when Tito defied Stalin he took on the role of a national leader, as he did when he led the resistance to Hitler. He put himself in the stream of Yugoslav history.

Stalin was in control of the Communist parties of other East European states, where he was completing the process of breaking the power of all non-Communist groups. In Yugoslavia it was Tito who had eliminated such groups without Stalin's help. He had a tightly organized Communist party, a loyal army of former partisans, a good intelligence system, an effective security police. He was incensed at Stalin's attempts to penetrate those organizations with Soviet agents, as he was at Soviet efforts to impose unequal economic relations on Yugoslavia and to make the Belgrade regime serve Soviet rather than Yugoslav interests. Stalin, in turn, was incensed at Tito's stubbornness and at his attempting to play a role in Eastern Europe that was not determined for him by Moscow. Stalin expressed indignation that the Yugoslav government had the nerve to treat the Soviet ambassador in Belgrade in the same way as the bourgeois ambassadors. Tito's spirit of independence was, in Stalin's eyes, insubordination.

Despite this clash of views and of wills, the decision to defy the Soviet Union and Stalin was one of tremendous psychological difficulty for the Yugoslav Communists. Tito himself had fought for communism in the Russian civil war. He had been a Comintern agent for years. The "movement," with its center in Moscow, had been his life. He and his lieutenants were convinced Communists. Many of them had fought in Spain in the 1930s. They had come through four years of tough partisan warfare for a cause they believed they shared with Stalin, who to them was liken unto a god. To pit their own decisions and their own will against his required great courage. But it also required surmounting a crisis of faith. It was the climax to a traumatic rethinking of the nature of the Communist movement and of the relations among Communist parties and states. Those in the movement, Russians and non-Russians, who had previously disagreed with or defied Stalin generally did not long survive. Tito and his colleagues knew that, and were prepared to take their chances.

It is often said that Tito did not break with the Soviet bloc,

that he was kicked out of it by Stalin. Strictly, that is true. The Cominform resolution expelled "the leaders of the Communist Party of Yugoslavia" from the family, and Tito continued to plead for the chance to argue his case, to establish the true facts before the other parties, and to prove that he was loyal to Leninism but had been misunderstood and wrongly treated. The fact remains that he was kicked out because, as the record shows, he would not take orders. It was his defiance that brought about the split.

It is now a cliché that unity in the Communist world was impossible to maintain once Communist rule was established in states beyond the frontiers of the Soviet Union; local Communist leaders, so the saying goes, inevitably had to adapt their policies to local conditions. But that proposition was not so crystal-clear in 1948. It was certainly not clear to Stalin, and Tito had no assurance he could get away with placing the interests of his own country above those of the fatherland of socialism. He was the one to make the first break in the monolith and to prove that it could be done. That was the real meaning of 1948.

### The American Reaction

That meaning was not immediately grasped in Washington. The first reaction, understandably, was astonishment. Communist leaders did not talk to each other in that way, at least not in public. Some Western observers of the Communist scene believed that the whole thing was a fraud, an act put on by Stalin and Tito to fool the world. The situation was both confused and confusing for the West, since Yugoslavia showed no open change in its generally hostile attitude toward non-Communist nations. At the international conference on Danube River navigation, which opened in Belgrade one month after the break, the Yugoslav delegates did all they could to show their solidarity with Moscow so far as East-West relations were concerned. At the Fifth Congress of the Yugoslav Communist party held in Belgrade in July, Tito had justified his defiance of Stalin, declared political war on the Cominform, burned his bridges behind him, and won a full vote of confidence. Yet the West could still regard this as some kind of private Communist quarrel, bringing no evident advantage to the free world.

Much credit is due the American Ambassador to Yugoslavia, Cavendish W. Cannon, and his staff for the way in which they handled an unprecedented situation. Cannon had been in Belgrade through the period when Yugoslav-American relations were at rock bottom, when his embassy was virtually under siege by the security police and diplomatic exchanges were little more than a series of protests, claims, and insults. He had won respect for his firmness and his diplomatic sense. Aware a short time before June 28 that something was wrong in Yugoslav-Soviet relations, the embassy fully grasped the meaning of what was happening in the days that followed. Without much encouragement from Washington in that early period, Ambassador Cannon saw the situation as one which presented for the first time opportunities for practical efforts toward a goal of American foreign policy which had been nothing but a hope, the weakening and eventual breakup of the Soviet bloc. He saw that the United States could not just sit back and watch this quarrel between Communists, because Yugoslavia was on the frontier of the East-West confrontation. If Stalin should win, the West would be worse off than before; if Tito should make good his defiance, it would be much better off. The question was whether the West, especially the United States, was going to do anything to influence the situation brought on by this most portentous heresy since that of Henry VIII.

Early in 1949 Washington adopted a policy based on the conclusions that Yugoslavia's break with the Soviet Union was real, that it was in the interest of the United States to see it continue, and that steps should be taken to that end. The first concrete embodiment of the new policy was a change in export-licensing procedures so that American goods could be exported to Yugoslavia without running into the obstacles put in the way of deliveries to other Communist countries. The precise action was not of great moment. The Yugoslav government had not made any appeal to Washington for help. The important fact was that the United States had deliberately chosen a course of helping a Communist country to maintain its independence.

The decision was less than wholehearted throughout the government. Secretary of Defense Louis Johnson, for example, held up for months the export of a steel mill which Yugoslavia had purchased, until the matter finally went to the President, who decided against him. The mill itself was not vital in Yugoslavia's immediate situation, but it was a symbol, a test of American intent.

As Stalin's pressure on Yugoslavia increased—denunciation by the Soviet Union and the East European states of their treaties of alliance with Yugoslavia, concentration of troops on Yugoslavia's frontiers, provocation of hundreds of border incidents, organization of groups of anti-Tito Yugoslavs in neighboring countries, a continuous barrage of propaganda calling for the overthrow of Tito's government, and an economic boycott that soon became complete—so also did Yugoslavia's desperation increase, and Tito's willingness to turn to the devil (in this case the capitalist West) for support. He began to mend some fences on his western borders. He sought more normal relations with Austria and Italy. He closed his frontier with Greece (where pro-Yugoslav elements among the Communists had already lost out), a step which, together with the increased military effort of the Greek armed forces, sealed the doom of the Communist rebellion in that country. He worked out new trade arrangements with Britain. And he requested a loan from the Export-Import Bank of Washington.

The first American loan to Yugoslavia, totaling $20 million, was announced in September 1949 as a normal business transaction. It was no secret that both governments regarded it as basically a political loan. Each would have liked to see it help tide Yugoslavia over the difficult period in which its economic plans were disrupted and its foreign trade had to be shifted from east to west. This was, in fact, far too large a problem to be solved by a loan of $20 million. Neither government, at this early stage, was comfortable in taking a public position of collaboration with the other. At the same time, they were feeling their way toward arrangements more commensurate with the dangers each saw in the prospect of the downfall of the Belgrade regime and the establishment of full Soviet control of Yugoslavia. That meant collaboration well beyond "normal business transactions."

At the session of the United Nations General Assembly in the fall of 1949, Yugoslavia put its case before the world, denouncing the Soviet Union for its aggressive actions. Thus, more than a year after the break, Yugoslav foreign policy was publicly unhooked from the Soviet line. The conflict could no longer be called a dispute between Communist parties of no concern to the outside world. It was a dispute between governments, and one of those governments was forcefully reiterating the point that the law of nations and especially the Charter of the United Nations applied to relations between Communist states as between any others.

The United States, in policy decisions taken at this time, made ready to extend more economic help to Yugoslavia if it should be needed and studied how Yugoslav resistance to a possible military attack might be strengthened. The question of a formal American undertaking to assist Yugoslavia in case of attack was never broached. Nevertheless, when George V. Allen, the newly named Ambassador to Yugoslavia, saw President Truman in December before leaving to take up his post, he made the following statement to the press:

> The President confirmed that the United States is unalterably opposed to aggression wherever it occurs or threatens to occur. Furthermore, the United States supports the principle of the sovereignty of independent nations. As regards Yugoslavia, we are just as opposed to aggression against that country as against any other, and just as favorable to the retention of Yugoslavia's sovereignty . . .[5]

This was not a statement carefully drafted in the State Department. That was just as well. With the bluntness characteristic of both Harry Truman and George Allen, it put the world, and especially the Soviet Union, on notice that the Soviet-Yugoslav dispute had become a part of the cold war, and thus that it held the danger of a real war between the big powers. It was not a commitment, but by explicitly including Yugoslavia within the scope of its basic foreign policies the United States went a long way toward throwing the mantle of a security guarantee over Tito's shoulders.

[5] *The New York Times,* December 24, 1949.

Stalin had not attacked Yugoslavia with military force at the time of the break because he did not think it necessary. "I will shake my little finger," Nikita Khrushchev later reported him as saying to his colleagues, "and there will be no more Tito. He will fall."[6] It was better to avoid the opprobrium of attacking a small country that had been an ally, since subversion and pressure would bring about the desired result. The Cominform, meeting in November 1949 in Hungary, issued an appeal to good Yugoslav Communists to overthrow the "fascist" regime of "the Tito clique." By that time, however, the expectation that this could actually be done was beginning to wear a little thin. Yet by that time, too, changing to military means was neither easy nor safe. Stalin could see, with the growing Western involvement in Yugoslavia, that an armed attack on that country might bring on a general war.

### The Reasons Behind American Policy

The American decision to support Tito's Yugoslavia was not made without initial hesitation, as we have seen. For the Tito-Stalin break came at a time when the United States was up to its ears in the cold war, which Americans generally regarded as a struggle not only against the Soviet Union but also against communism. That not much distinction was made between the two was natural when we were engaged in Greece against Greek Communists supported by the Communist governments of Albania, Yugoslavia, and Bulgaria; when we had just seen local Communists with Soviet backing destroy coalition regimes in Poland, Hungary and Czechoslavakia; when we were helping democratic governments in France and Italy to defend themselves against Communist strikes and violence. In such an atmosphere it was not easy to rush to the aid of a Communist government which had been a partner in that campaign against the United States and its allies.

[6] "Secret Speech" of February 25-26, 1956, text released by U.S. Department of State, published as *The Anatomy of Terror, Khrushchev's Revelations About Stalin's Regime*, Introduction by Nathaniel Weyl (Washington: Public Affairs Press, 1956), p. 55.

The reasons of self-interest for the United States and the entire West, however, were so clear that any other course would have been a triumph of ideological fervor over good sense. The Western governments saw no chance of a democratic, Western-type regime emerging from Yugoslavia's crisis. The alternatives were two: the Tito regime or a Cominform regime controlled by Stalin. Thus, if the Western nations were going to support Yugoslavia, they would have to provide their assistance to a Communist government. They made that choice.

In the first place, as Hamilton Fish Armstrong noted, "the break between Belgrade and Moscow transformed the military strategy of Europe and necessitated changes in the plans of every Power which might become engaged in hostilities there."[7] The strategic advantages to the West of the existence of a truly independent Yugoslavia were undeniable. When Yugoslavia was an ally of the Soviet Union, whether or not Soviet troops were stationed on Yugoslav soil, the military power of the Soviet bloc pressed on the borders of Italy and reached the whole eastern shore of the Adriatic. With Yugoslavia independent, that line was moved back to the middle of the Balkan Peninsula, Albania was cut off geographically from the rest of the bloc, and pressure on Italy and Greece was relieved. Furthermore, Tito's army of thirty-three divisions, the strongest in Eastern Europe, could be subtracted from the total forces of the bloc and in certain circumstances might be engaged against the Soviet Union on the side of the West. With Belgrade's cooperation, Italy might be defended at its natural line of defense, the Ljubljana Gap in northern Yugoslavia, instead of on the Venetian plain, and Greece might be defended in the upper Vardar valley instead of at Salonika. Yugoslavia was the missing link in the eastern flank of Western defense. If it were not hostile, even if no more than neutral, that was a great gain.

On the political side the reasons were less clear but in the long run possibly more significant. That the Soviet empire could be moved backward from an important area, not through military action by the West but through the decision of the government of the area in question, was a portentous fact. The arguments

[7] *Tito and Goliath* (New York: Macmillan, 1951), p. 284.

Tito was advancing struck at the heart of the system which had made the Communist world so formidable, a system of unity in which the relations and policies of the member states were determined on the basis of the supremacy of the party line decided at the center. Tito's case rested on the principle of sovereign equality of socialist states, which Moscow had preached for propaganda purposes but never practised. It was an obvious interest of the West to encourage the Yugoslavs in that line of thought and to help Tito make his argument stick. His successful resistance would enable Communist Yugoslavia to be independent *of* the Soviet bloc, even though his original intention had been to be independent *within* it. If he failed, Stalin would have a resounding political victory and a regime of his own choosing in Belgrade.

The third main reason behind American support of Tito was precisely this possibility of basic change in the nature of the relations among Communist states. In all of the satellite Communist parties the divisive issue of the relative weight to be given national concerns as opposed to those of international communism as determined in Moscow was present or latent. In some cases it was reflected in differences between those leaders whose earlier years had been spent largely in the Soviet Union and those who had served the cause at home, mainly in jail and in the wartime resistance. The latter might be expected to be attracted by Titoism, which would enable their countries to become independent while remaining Communist. But any Western hopes that other East European states would soon follow Yugoslavia's example were doomed to disappointment. The conditions which made Yugoslavia's defection possible did not then exist in the rest of Stalin's empire.

Tito and his partisans had fought a long war against the Germans and, although helped in the closing stages by the Red Army, were not beholden to the Soviet Union for their control of the country. Tito had an army, a tightly organized party, and a police apparatus, all loyal to him, not to the Soviet Union or Stalin. He was therefore able to take swift and drastic action against "Cominformists," Stalin's potential fifth column.

Yugoslavia, moreover, had a geographical position that held

realistic possibilities for defense and for economic support from the West. The leaders of other East European states could not have followed Tito even if they had wished to do so. Their countries were under Soviet military occupation or control. Their armies, police establishments, and governmental bureaucracies were honeycombed with Soviet officers, agents, and advisers. Communist parties like those in Hungary or Rumania had no roots in the people and needed Soviet support to maintain their new power. Besides, Stalin took the Tito affair as the signal for a series of purges in the satellite parties that swept Titoists and potential Titoists out of positions of influence and sent some of them to their graves as traitors to socialism. The satellite regimes, their cooperation assured by this drastic action, were mobilized to carry on the war of nerves and the economic offensive against Yugoslavia. Among the weapons brought into play were old territorial claims and aspirations of which nothing had been heard on the official level since the "fraternal" Communist parties came into power at the end of the war and declared such problems solved.

Actually, it was Titoism's significance for the future rather than its immediate possibilities that counted. Among the leaders purged for Titoism was the Polish Communist, Wladyslaw Gomulka, who had the good fortune not to be executed, as were his counterparts in other East European states. Yugoslavia's example was not lost on other Communists, although the effect was often latent and not immediately apparent. In the Western world the magnitude of the challenge to international communism as a monolithic system was perhaps more fully grasped by Europeans than by Americans. The United States government therefore did not make this point the main reason for its policy of helping Tito, although officials in the Department of State were well aware of the significance of successful heresy in the Communist world. For the military, the Congress, and the public the more telling argument was the strategic shift on the map.

It was of some importance to Tito's playing the role of heretic that he keep his position as a Communist or socialist, thwarting Stalin's attempt to pin on him the label of fascist and lackey of the imperialists. Cooperation with the West, he said privately to

American officials and publicly to the world, was acceptable only on the basis of no political demands and no political concessions so far as Yugoslavia's socialist system was concerned. Although many in the United States did not like that idea and wished to see the American aid used as a means of forcing the regime to give more rights to the people of Yugoslavia, the U.S. government, wisely, made no attempt to impose conditions of that nature. Frequently, however, it had occasion to draw the attention of Yugoslav officials to American public concern over such matters as persecution of religion and the holding of political prisoners, and to remind them that the Congress, which had the ultimate word on appropriating funds for aid to Yugoslavia, was responsive to public opinion. Certain measures of leniency which the Yugoslav government then took, on its own, showed that the message got across.

American officials were not averse to letting the Yugoslavs know that this country had not changed its views on such questions as free elections and human rights, which had been the subject of so many of its statements before June 28, 1948. Ambassador Allen frankly told audiences in both countries that we did not like the Yugoslav system of government any more than the Yugoslav leaders liked ours. But policy was something else. Policy toward Yugoslavia was based on a cold-blooded calculation of self-interest on both sides. The mutual need for cooperation in the present was self-evident. As to the longer-term future, each retained its reservations and its hopes. On the American side there was at least some expectation that the mere fact of growing economic, cultural, and military relations would inevitably tend to draw Yugoslavia toward the West and to encourage changes at home, almost in spite of the regime's wishes.

### Aid Policy in Full Bloom

Informally, American aid to Yugoslavia was described as a policy of "keeping Tito afloat." That is to say, it did not represent an attempt to include Yugoslavia in any general plan for European recovery, to raise its living standards, or to ensure the success of its current five-year plan. It consisted of a series of emergency measures to help Yugoslavia avoid economic difficulties that would undermine its capacity to maintain independence no matter how firm the political will of its leaders might be.

In 1948, about half of Yugoslavia's foreign trade was with the Soviet bloc. Then, abruptly, the former brother nations broke off trade agreements, suspended promised credits, cut off vital supplies of fuel and other goods, and applied a general boycott and blockade. The Yugoslavs had to reorient their foreign trade, find new sources of supply, and gain credits from the West, all in a brief period of time. The West responded first with stopgap measures to prevent an economic collapse, then with a number of trade agreements, loans, and grants aimed at helping Yugoslavia to cover its balance-of-payments deficit until it had made the necessary adjustments in its economy and could be expected to make its own way. Even those limited aims led to a volume of aid not dreamed of in the early period following the decision to "keep Tito afloat."

By the spring of 1950 the Export-Import Bank had extended two loans totaling $40 million. But as spring turned into a hot, dry summer on the Yugoslav plains, it became apparent that the country was in the grip of a drought which, combined with an agricultural policy that had antagonized the peasants, threatened a national disaster. The Yugoslav leaders finally came to the point of officially requesting grant aid from the United States to meet the emergency. The Yugoslav request and the American response represented a vital turning point for both countries.

Prior aid had gone to Yugoslavia by decisions of the Executive Branch: through administration of trade controls, action by the Export-Import Bank, and some ingenious interpretation of the existing aid legislation.[8] There was no aid agreement, which was a requirement for Marshall Plan aid. In the fall of 1950 the administration decided to face the issue squarely and go to Congress. That was one of the reasons for President Truman's calling the Eighty-first Congress back for a special session in November.

[8] The administration, in November 1950, made available $15 million, under the Mutual Defense Assistance Act, for food which would go nominally to the Yugoslav armed forces. It also made arrangements during the same month to transfer to Yugoslavia $11.5 million worth of flour, then stored in Germany and Italy under the European Recovery Act. Part of a third Export-Import Bank loan of $15 million was diverted to food purchases.

Basing his request on both political and humanitarian grounds, the President asked for emergency funds to help rescue the Yugoslav people from threatened famine. He frankly set forth the factors which had already led the Executive Branch to come to the support of Yugoslavia. Key members of both houses were convinced by his reasoning and especially by the strategic argument. They knew that more than charity was involved. Those thirty-three Yugoslav divisions standing opposed to the Soviet forces were persuasive. No strong opposition developed in the Congress or in the country, despite some concern about strengthening a Communist regime. The Yugoslav Emergency Relief Act of 1950, authorizing the expenditure of $50 million, was passed by a vote of 60 to 21 in the Senate and by 225 to 142 in the House.[9]

This act of the legislature, in effect a declaration of support for existing government policy, cleared the air. Aid to Yugoslavia had gained a new respectability. Henceforward the administration felt able to go ahead with the inclusion of Yugoslavia in the regular appropriations of the Economic Cooperation Administration (ECA), and also to coordinate American aid with that of other Western nations. In the spring of 1951 the United States, Britain, and France worked out a tripartite grant program to cover Yugoslavia's anticipated balance-of-payments gap in the coming year, and agreed to coordinate their dealings with Yugoslavia through economic missions in Belgrade. Discussions were held with Yugoslavia's other creditors, especially West Germany, so that the burden of repaying loans would be spread out and thus lightened. With this much assurance that Yugoslavia was a good credit risk, the World Bank went ahead in October 1951 with a $28 million loan which had been under discussion with the Yugoslavs since 1949.[10] "Keeping Tito afloat" had become a common policy of the Western world.

Military aid was a more delicate question to handle, but it was, like economic aid, a natural outcome of the basic policy

[9] These were the votes on the bills initially before the two houses. Because of amendments the two bills were not identical and were sent to conference. The agreed bill reported out of the conference was accepted by both houses without a recorded vote. See *Congressional Record*, 81st Cong., 2d sess., vol. 96, Part 12, pp. 16402-3, 16547, and 16738-42.

[10] The Bank made available a second *tranche* of $30 million in 1953.

decisions taken both in Belgrade and in the major capitals of the West. In 1949 and 1950, as the Soviet Union concentrated its own and satellite military forces on Yugoslavia's frontiers and made other threatening moves, the Yugoslavs had to prepare to meet an attack and to look for new sources of military equipment. At the same time the United States, after the attack on South Korea in June 1950, expected that the same pattern of aggression by satellite forces might well be repeated against Yugoslavia. When a Yugoslav emissary made discreet soundings late in that same year, Washington was receptive.

During the following months some limited amounts of American supplies arrived in Yugoslavia. Not the quantity but the fact of their arrival was important. To the Yugoslavs, and to Moscow, it was a timely sign, in a form that could not be mistaken, of the commitment of American power to Yugoslavia's defense. Later in 1951, as a result of informal discussions which American representatives had with Britain, France and Canada, odd lots of miscellaneous equipment (old World War II stocks, German matériel, Soviet arms captured in Korea, and such) were turned up to meet the emergency. But again, as with economic aid, a half-secret, improvised, and legally questionable way of meeting the problem was not satisfactory. The U.S. government saw the need of facing the question squarely and telling the Yugoslavs that they too must do so. If they wanted usable equipment in any quantity, they could get it only through the Mutual Defense Assistance Program, which required a public finding by the President that Yugoslavia was "of direct importance to the defense of the North Atlantic area," and that its increased ability to defend itself was "important . . . to the security of the United States."[11]

[11] Public Law 621, 81st Cong., 2d sess., "To amend the Mutual Defense Assistance Act of 1949," July 26, 1950, had required a presidential finding that aid could be provided to a European nation, other than NATO members and Greece and Turkey, "whose strategic location makes it of direct importance to the defense of the North Atlantic area and whose immediately increased ability to defend itself . . . contributes to the preservation of the peace and security of the North Atlantic area and is vital to the security of the United States." Some economic aid was extended, nominally for the use of Yugoslavia's armed forces, under this law. The subsequent legislation, the Mutual Security Act of 1951 (Public Law 165, 82nd Cong., 1st sess., October 10, 1951), under which the military aid agreement with Yugoslavia was negotiated, contained substantially the same provision but substituted "important" for "vital."

It also required the signing of a bilateral Mutual Defense Assistance Program (MDAP) agreement and the acceptance of a U.S. Military Assistance Advisory Group (MAAG) in Belgrade.

Ambassador Allen was well cast in the role of manager of a new kind of American policy, just as Ambassador Cannon had been suited to the tasks of the transition period. Yugoslavia now wanted American aid, badly, and the United States wanted to provide it. But it was by no means easy to turn that general disposition on both sides into actual cooperation. Suspicion remained thick, as both groped toward mutually acceptable and effective working relations. Allen skillfully negotiated both the ECA and MDAP agreements, which had to depart from the usual language used for other recipient nations because of Yugoslavia's special position and susceptibilities; yet they still contained many clauses, required under the aid legislation, which Tito surprised American negotiators by accepting without argument. The way of the U.S. aid mission in Belgrade and especially of the MAAG was never smooth, but they did their job well and won the confidence of Yugoslav officials. The purpose of both governments, to pull Yugoslavia through a critical period without military attack or economic disaster, was achieved.

It seemed quite possible, moreover, that cooperation would move beyond that minimum purpose. In the United Nations, Yugoslavia came to play what was, from the Western viewpoint at least, an ever more constructive role. The United States supported Yugoslavia for the "East European" seat on the Security Council in 1949, and it was elected over Soviet opposition. In 1950 Yugoslavia voted for the "Uniting for Peace" resolution, which enabled the General Assembly to recommend collective action in case of aggression despite a Soviet veto in the Security Council. The American and Yugoslav delegations worked closely together in winning support for the resolution, passed by the General Assembly in 1951, which expressed "serious concern" over the pressures exerted on Yugoslavia by the Soviet Union and other Cominform states, and called for the normalization of Soviet-Yugoslav relations. In the economic field, the tripartite U.S.-British-French grant aid program was continued through 1952-53, but thereafter the United States, with Yugoslav cooperation, carried on alone. On the military side, General J. Lawton Collins, Chief of Staff of the U.S. Army, visited Yugoslavia in 1951 and thereupon became a champion of Yugoslavia in the Pentagon. The military aid program, growing in volume, was directed largely to equipping those Yugoslav divisions stationed in the area of the Ljubljana Gap, the key point for the defense of Italy. Plans were made for direct Yugoslav-Italian military talks and for bilateral Yugoslav-American talks on strategy. In February 1953, Yugoslavia signed with Greece and Turkey a treaty of friendship and cooperation. Yugoslavia seemed to be edging toward an informal participation in the NATO system of defense against the Soviet Union.

In March 1953 came the news that Stalin had died. No one in Belgrade or in Washington knew what the change in Soviet leadership might portend. Although there was no immediate sign that Soviet determination to unseat the "Tito clique" had flagged, the Yugoslavs took a more cautious attitude on military negotiations with the United States. The planned talks on strategy never took place, and there was reason to doubt that the Yugoslav leaders would ever let their military plans and dispositions be determined in the framework of general defense of Western Europe rather than on the basis of their own national defense. Nevertheless, they did go ahead with negotiations to turn their entente with Greece and Turkey into a military pact, signed in August 1954, providing mutual guarantees against attack and taking into account the NATO obligations of the other two partners. They reached a settlement with Italy on Trieste in October 1954 through the helpful diplomacy of the United States and Britain. Both events were notable successes for Western diplomacy and were warmly welcomed in Belgrade. Yugoslav-American cooperation continued as before, while American aid programs, now well established, gathered momentum.

### The Price Tag

Let us look at the total amounts of aid, which did so much to bring about these favorable results. The time period taken is from mid-1949 through mid-1955, the period of continuing Soviet pressure and of successful Yugoslav resistance. The United States extended $55 million in loans on fairly easy terms. The food relief law of 1950 authorized a grant of $50 million. From MDAP funds and later from the regular foreign aid program (ECA and successor agencies) U.S. grants came to $356 million. Surplus food shipments amounted to $49.5 million in sales for local currency and $88 million in grants. Although grants, loans, and sales are not truly comparable, the total of $598.5 million from all sources gives a rough idea of the value of goods Yugoslavia received.[12]

The amount of military aid is more difficult to determine, partly because dollar values put on various kinds of less-than-new equipment are often arbitrary. Official government figures, however, give us a good general measure of how big the Yugoslav program was. They show a total of $588.5 million up to mid-1955.[13]

Thus, considering military and economic aid together, the United States paid out nearly $1.2 billion, of which only $55 million was to come back in the form of repaid loans. Was this too high a price to pay? It is scarcely possible to put a monetary price on a political gain or loss. One cannot even say for certain that it was American aid that saved Yugoslavia's independence, though many who were involved in the events of the day have little doubt that it did.[14] The critical period, without much doubt, was from 1949 through 1951. The emergency assistance given then with the firm assurance of more to come, at a time when the Yugoslav leaders were feeling the full heat of Stalin's pressure, was crucial. The larger amounts provided in the next three or

[12] See Appendix Table, p. 171, below.

[13] Agency for International Development, *U.S. Foreign Assistance and Assistance from International Organizations, Obligations and Loan Authorizations, July 1, 1945–June 30, 1962,* (Washington: GPO, 1962), p. 126.

[14] Occasional official Yugoslav statements have recognized its importance, but most accounts written for internal consumption mention it only in passing and stress the "heavy burden" which the terms of Western aid represented for Yugoslavia (though in fact the greater part was in grants, and loan terms were readjusted in Yugoslavia's favor). See, for example, the semi-official short history of the League of Communists, *Pregled Istorije Saveza Komunista Jugoslavije* (Belgrade: Institut za Izučavanje Radničkog Pokreta, 1963), pp. 500-501.

four years were less so, but they helped to consolidate what was a real victory both for Yugoslavia and for the West. The United States could certainly "afford" the billion dollars, even taking account of its other heavy obligations. Indeed, it was a small price to pay for what was the one strikingly successful policy the United States was able to conduct in Eastern Europe during the whole period since the war.

## Chapter III

# 1955: The Reconciliation

Stalin's successors inherited his policy of excommunication of Yugoslavia. None seems to have opposed it during his lifetime, but it was not long in becoming a matter of controversy among them after his death. As with a whole range of questions affecting Soviet internal affairs and foreign relations, they were bound to review a policy which had been a spectacular failure. It was a readily apparent fact that Tito had survived the most severe pressures the Soviet Union and its satellites could apply—short of military force, which they had not attempted and now certainly would not. Meanwhile, Tito's continuing challenge to Soviet prestige in the Communist world was an abiding nuisance. Stalin had not succeeded in making people believe that fascism had been installed in Yugoslavia, and Tito kept reminding them that what Yugoslavia was building was socialism, whatever anyone else chose to call it, and that though he accepted Western aid he gave not even the shadow of a political concession for it. The idea dawned upon some of the Soviet leaders that if Soviet policy was futile and embarrassing, maybe it ought to be changed.

Tito's terms for reconciliation were on the record. The Soviet Union would have to establish normal relations with Yugoslavia as an independent state. Nothing like the old relationship or those prevailing between the Soviet Union and its East European satellites would be acceptable. Without taking any decision to agree to those terms, the new Soviet leaders began to show signs of wanting to make relations a little less glacial. In the summer of 1953 they proposed an exchange of ambassadors (there had been none since 1948 though diplomatic relations had never been broken), and Belgrade agreed. Frontier incidents fell off. The barrage of propaganda slackened. Some of Yugoslavia's eastern neighbors took the initiative to restore traffic and more normal procedures on the borders. In 1954 some of the bloc countries and finally the Soviet Union itself concluded economic agreements with Belgrade. Then in November, Khrushchev and other high Soviet officials appeared at the national holiday reception at the Yugoslav embassy in Moscow, where they lifted their glasses in a toast to "Comrade" Tito.

The Yugoslav leaders looked on these developments with a certain satisfaction, but retained their skepticism. They reassured the West that they would not fall into any trap, and that moves toward better relations with the East did not mean a reduction in friendship with others. Those moves were paralleled, as we have noted, by Yugoslavia's conclusion of the Balkan Pact, the agreement on Trieste, and the continuance of close working relationships with the West.

That there would be any basic change in Soviet policy toward Yugoslavia could not easily be deduced from Foreign Minister Molotov's comprehensive foreign policy speech in February 1955. He expressed the hope for better relations but said that its realization depended on Yugoslavia no less than on the Soviet Union. Nevertheless, he did say that Yugoslavia's drift from positions taken in the period immediately after the Second World War was "exclusively her internal affair."[1] Then, one fine day in May, it was announced to the world that a Soviet delegation including Premier Bulganin, Khrushchev, Mikoyan, and Gromyko would make a governmental visit to Belgrade.

Despite the signs of thaw which had gone before, the news that such a group of the top governmental and party leadership—with the conspicuous absence of Molotov—was about to descend on the capital of a small country until recently the object of its vituperation and hostility was a bombshell. The Yugoslav lead-

---

[1] Report to the Supreme Soviet of the USSR, February 8, 1955, *New Times*, no. 7, February 12, 1955, Supplement, p. 23.

ers, who had received and agreed to the proposal only a short time before, sensed a major political victory in the offing. Those in Washington who concerned themselves with Yugoslav affairs had been prepared for additional moves toward normal Soviet-Yugoslav relations, but not for this. Reaction in the corridors of the State Department, which got the word from Belgrade only at the last minute before it became public, ranged from "We've had it" to a more hopeful "Let's wait and see." The conviction that Yugoslavia could never return to the Soviet fold was, to say the least, shaken.

### The Declaration of Belgrade

American observers watched with interest and some anxiety the drama of the Soviet delegation's visit: the scene at the Belgrade airport where Khrushchev advanced with a beaming smile on "Comrade" Tito to assure him that the evil policies of the past—all the fault of Beria and Abakumov (read: Stalin)—were over, and Tito, stiffly formal, silently motioned his ebullient guest to a waiting Rolls Royce; the arduous negotiating sessions interspersed with trips to farm and factory; Khrushchev's clowning and informality which provided good copy for the newsmen and gave a bizarre tone to the social occasions; and the final production, the Declaration of Belgrade signed by Tito and by Bulganin, not Khrushchev, for this was a governmental and not a party agreement. All was not free and easy in the communication between the two groups, but the salient fact emerged that this was the beginning of a new era in Soviet-Yugoslav relations and in Yugoslavia's position in the world. Above all, it was a great triumph for Tito. For the Soviet leaders, although they saw it as an opening wedge for later political gains, the trip to Belgrade was a trip to Canossa. Khrushchev, although he did not act like a humble penitent, was setting the seal on the humiliation of a great power by a small one. The Yugoslavs had stood firm, and they had won.

The Belgrade Declaration formally confirmed the Yugoslav position on separate roads to socialism. It contained statements of general agreement on numerous questions of international policy—on Germany, China, disarmament, and others—but Yugoslav positions were already similar to Moscow's on those matters. The real significance of the declaration lay in Soviet acceptance of Titoism, enshrined in a number of principles, including "respect for the sovereignty, independence, integrity and for equality among states in their mutual relations and in their relations with other states," and "mutual respect for, and non-interference in, internal affairs for any reason whatsoever, whether of an economic, political or ideological nature, because questions of internal organization, or difference in social systems and of different forms of Socialist development, are solely the concern of the individual countries."[2]

How the declaration would be interpreted by both sides was a matter for the future. The Soviet leaders had their own good reasons for accepting the bargain. Though ceding on principle, they had undoubtedly gained in tactical advantages over the previous position. They had checked what seemed to be a drift by Yugoslavia toward the Western camp. They had restored communications with Belgrade and opened up possibilities which could lead in time to a reassertion of Soviet influence and domination.

### Dulles and Tito

These possibilities the United States had to assess in making an estimate of Yugoslavia's position and a reappraisal of its own aims and policies, including the whole panoply of military and economic aid. Had Yugoslavia moved toward the Soviet side to the point where the reasons underlying American aid were no longer valid? Put another way, as a state enjoying normal and even friendly relations with the Soviet Union, was Yugoslavia of the same importance to the United States as when, a prospective object of Soviet attack, it had been leaning on the West for support? These questions were discussed in Washington with James Riddleberger, the American Ambassador to Yugoslavia,

[2] Robert Bass and Elizabeth Marbury (eds.), *The Soviet-Yugoslav Controversy, 1948-58: A Documentary Record* (New York: Prospect Books, 1959), pp. 55-60.

and brought before the National Security Council. The conclusion reached was that the vital point remained unchanged: Yugoslavia's determination to be independent. Riddleberger put it too simply when he told the press that "nothing is really changed in the relationship of Yugoslavia with the West."[3] However, the United States and the West would continue to benefit from Yugoslavia's new middle position, although it was far less reassuring than having Moscow and Belgrade at swords' points with each other. The Yugoslav army could still be considered a factor on the Western side in the military balance, as it would defend its own country if attacked from the East, even if unwilling to enter into military collaboration with the West. Yugoslavia's economic health was still important to the West as a buttress of the country's independent position. For these reasons it was decided to keep on with both military and economic aid.

This was not an easy decision for Secretary Dulles to make. He was having his fill of "neutralists" in Bandung, New Delhi, Cairo, and elsewhere who seemed to be primarily engaged in attacking American positions and interests to the benefit of the Communist powers, and Tito had begun to build up an informal association with them. A few weeks after the Soviet delegation's visit, Nehru went to Belgrade to state his "close identity of views" with Tito. But Dulles's main concern about Yugoslavia in the year 1955 had to do with its role in Europe. It was the year of Soviet agreement on the Austrian state treaty, of the summit conference and the subsequent Foreign Ministers' meeting in Geneva, of a serious effort to get a settlement on Germany. Dulles saw more to be gained by stressing and encouraging Yugoslavia's independence, which could still have a disruptive influence on the Soviet empire, than in writing it off on the general principle (proclaimed by himself) that neutralism was immoral. Communism was also immoral, but a Communist state turned neutralist was far better for America's interests, and presumably more moral, than a Soviet satellite.

American policy to continue aid to Yugoslavia was already set when Secretary Dulles came to visit Tito in November 1955 at Brioni, his Adriatic island retreat, during a lull in the Foreign

[3] *The New York Times,* June 16, 1955.

Ministers' conference at Geneva. This meeting of the former Comintern agent and the austere Calvinist layman and Wall Street lawyer, to whom communism was evil in itself, was not without its drama. On the great issues of the world's future, as on the interpretation of its past, they had no common ground. Each, however, could see the considerations of hard national interest that motivated the other, and both saw the advantages of continued cooperation.

The Secretary set the tone of his visit in a message to "the people of Yugoslavia" even before he left Geneva. He cited "Yugoslavia's fight to win and keep its independence" as a dramatic chapter of history. "Your country has more than once made it clear that it will be no one's satellite. We applaud this stand." So far so good. Then he added, "You want to be independent, prosperous, and free to choose your government. That is what we Americans also want for Yugoslavia."[4] The Tito regime was also for Yugoslavia's independence. But it was not for the freedom of the Yugoslav people to choose their own government. The Yugoslav press, at the same time that it welcomed close cooperation with the United States, took pains to praise Yugoslavia's consistency in preserving and developing the ideas of the Great October Revolution, as well as the Soviet Union's break with the errors of the past and its positive contributions to the cause of peace and socialism.

The real differences appeared in the contretemps that came to the surface over Eastern Europe. On emerging from his talks with Tito, Dulles talked to the press as follows: "We reached common accord on recognizing the importance of independence for these States [of Eastern Europe], noninterference from the outside in their internal affairs, and their right to develop their own social and economic order in ways of their own choice."[5] These words could be interpreted according to the Dulles way of thinking as signifying support for self-determination in Eastern Europe, which meant a free popular choice for or against communism. Or they could be interpreted along Tito's line of thought: that the East European nations were becoming increasingly independent

[4] Radio Belgrade, Home Service, November 5, 1955.
[5] *Department of State Bulletin,* November 21, 1955, p. 833.

under their existing socialist regimes, and that the task ahead was to encourage them to move further in that direction.

Tito chose not to associate himself with the Secretary's precise words. He wanted it understood that Yugoslavia did not subscribe to any "liberation" intended to restore the old order in Eastern Europe, and that Yugoslav policies were consistent with the Belgrade Declaration. If Dulles and Tito agreed, wrote an authoritative Yugoslav commentator, it did not mean that Yugoslavia was giving up the principles it had held. The accord on the principle of self-determination was sincere, "although it is possible that the two statesmen would not agree on the very process of development, if it should be discussed, which was not the case at Brioni."[6]

The United States, by the Secretary's visit, showed that it was willing to treat Yugoslavia's position with respect. For both sides the meeting was a useful diplomatic gesture. On the other hand, the general American reassessment of Yugoslavia's position and of the consequences flowing from it tended to be oversimplified. So great was Washington's relief and satisfaction over the fact of Yugoslavia's continued independence and determination to defend it that the conclusion for the United States was to continue the same kind of policies and relationships as before, in the expectation of the same general cooperation. Yet such an expectation was hardly justified.

### The New Atmosphere

Yugoslav acceptance of American aid and the political collaboration that went with it had been a direct consequence of the regime's critical needs at a time when it was under siege from the east. The two governments were *de facto* allies in the respective cold wars in which each was engaged against the Soviet Union. If Yugoslavia needed weapons to deter attack, to get them from the only available source was worth a promise to use them to arm its divisions in the area of the Ljubljana Gap. To obtain food and raw materials desperately needed to keep the

[6] J. Arnejc, "After the Brioni Talks," *Review of International Affairs* (Belgrade), November 16, 1955, pp. 9-10.

economy going was absolutely necessary, even if one had to listen to American advice and permit a check on how the items were used. To have a virtual American commitment to defend Yugoslav independence, it was worthwhile to work together on some questions with the Western powers in the United Nations. But now the siege was lifted. Yugoslavia did not wish to lose what it had gained in the West. It certainly did not wish to lose all American aid. In its new bargaining position as a country between the blocs and able to deal with both, it could be more assertive of its own views and interests. It could be less concerned with Western desires and susceptibilities.

At the same time, there was now a real difference of view on the nature of Soviet policy in Europe. The United States stuck to its conviction that there had been no basic change in Soviet policy: that it was Khrushchev's aim to extend Soviet power into Central and Western Europe, as it had been Stalin's; in any case, it was prudent to hold that assumption until it was proved wrong. It followed that the states in the path of Soviet ambition, including Yugoslavia, had a common interest in maintaining and improving their defense.

Tito and his colleagues, on the other hand, took the interpretation that Soviet policy, including foreign policy, was changing quite rapidly. They gave most of the credit for it to Khrushchev, whom they pictured as the world's best hope for the Russian future, struggling against the Kremlin's remaining Stalinists. Had Khrushchev not shown that his talk of peaceful coexistence was more than an empty slogan by concluding the Austrian treaty, giving up the Soviet base in Finland, and making the pilgrimage to Belgrade? Military blocs were still a danger to peace, so ran the argument, but the Soviet Union was no longer threatening to attack anybody, and surely not Yugoslavia. Whether or not this line of thinking was more strongly presented in Yugoslav public statements than fixed in the minds of the leaders, it was almost immediately apparent in attitudes toward the West. NATO, which they had previously accepted as a necessary bulwark of peace in Europe, they now began to criticize as an aggressive anti-Communist bloc perpetuating the spirit of the cold war.

Combined with these new interpretations of Soviet and Western policies was a sense of exhilaration at the end of isolation from the Communist world. Without being taken in by the "fraternal solidarity" which had been the disguise for Soviet domination in the old days, the Yugoslav leaders could not help enjoying the prestige of acceptance again as a socialist state. By 1956, they were ready to proceed to the re-establishment of party contacts and greater intimacy and collaboration, especially after Khrushchev, at the Twentieth Congress of the Soviet Communist party, denounced Stalin, confirmed the liquidation of the abnormal relationship with Yugoslavia, and endorsed the doctrine of separate roads to socialism. Two months later the Cominform was dissolved, and in June Tito made a triumphant visit to Moscow. All this was heady wine for those who had so recently been reviled as "bootlickers of the imperialists" and "traitors to socialism," although they took care not to drink too much of it.

Perhaps Washington underestimated the relief felt by the Yugoslav regime at ending its exclusive reliance on the West. The association had been profitable for Yugoslavia; indeed, it had probably saved the country's independence. But the leaders had never felt comfortable in the relationship and were even fearful of exposure to the West without any political and ideological counterweight in the East. They learned some facts to temper or replace many of their ideological myths. They discovered that the West's price for help was not the sacrifice of their independence. But the ultimate purpose had been not to join the Western camp but to bring the Soviet leaders to their senses. When they had accomplished that, they could put their relations with the United States on a new basis.

Special military relationships were bound to be among the casualties of the changed atmosphere. Yugoslavia's pact with Greece and Turkey, two NATO members, became a dead letter as a military alliance, thanks partly to the outbreak of the Cyprus dispute but also to the cooler Yugoslav attitude. The Yugoslav regime chafed under its position of dependence on the United States for arms, albeit glad enough to get them; pressures from the East had slackened, and the annual round of criticism in the U.S. Congress, when the program came up each year for renewal, was less patiently received. The Yugoslav authorities made it more and more difficult for the U.S. military advisory group to perform its assigned functions, and finally in 1957 Tito terminated the American military aid program as no longer needed; in future, Yugoslavia would buy the equipment it required. The United States would have been in a more dignified position if it had itself taken the initiative to end military aid.

Economic aid was another matter. Tito did not regard the continuance of grant assistance from the United States as compromising Yugoslavia's new "nonaligned" position. His government had come to rely on it, as a means of meeting the now chronic annual deficit in Yugoslavia's international balance of payments. On the American side, its continuance seemed logical as proof that there had been no change in the conviction that Yugoslavia's independence should be supported and that its economic ties with the West should be strengthened. There was no longer the urgency of the early 1950s, which had made Western aid seem so necessary on both sides that neither was inclined to question it or to talk of conditions. Tito was now definitely "afloat" on his own, the common political purpose was less evident, and both sides had more flexibility. Yugoslavia used that flexibility, much as other neutralist states did, as one part of a bargaining system whereby it kept aid coming from both East and West without being beholden to either. The United States was less concerned with extracting tangible advantage, but it could and did attempt to use its aid to impress on the Yugoslavs the need for keeping a balance; and in this respect it was aided by their own knowledge that the East was no substitute for the West as an economic partner.

### The Second Soviet-Yugoslav Break

A test of both Yugoslav and American policy came again with a series of events in the late 1950s that rubbed much of the gloss off the re-establishment of normal and friendly relations between Belgrade and Moscow. To understand the ups and downs and occasional weird gyrations in those relations, it is necessary to go back to the famous Belgrade Declaration of 1955. Significant as it was in ending the Kremlin's cold war against Yugoslavia, it had covered up basic differences of interpretation and of principle.

Tito and his colleagues accepted the reconcilation, the renewed party contacts, and the restoration of economic relations as recognition of the rightness of the principles for which they had held out. Yugoslavia's separate road meant just that, freedom to build its own institutions and an equal and independent status in all relations with the Soviet Union and its allies, as with countries outside the Soviet bloc. Khrushchev, on the other hand, never gave up the idea of Yugoslavia's eventual return to the fold. That did not mean a return to a Stalinist empire, which no longer existed, but to the new and somewhat looser system that was taking shape in Eastern Europe. The leading role, of course, would still be Moscow's.

Tito had no trouble in distinguishing fact from fiction. He saw that forces were at work undermining Soviet control in certain countries of Eastern Europe. But he saw also that none of those states enjoyed, or was likely to be allowed to enjoy, the independence that Yugoslavia had. He applauded the directions of Soviet policy under Khrushchev, but the Soviet bloc was still a bloc and still under Soviet control, and Yugoslavia would not be a part of it.

The course of Soviet-Yugoslav relations from 1955 to 1960 reflected the interplay of the trend of reconciliation and the residue of basic conflict. In mid-1956 the Soviet leaders welcomed Tito to the Soviet Union, hailed him as a hero, and applauded the burgeoning fraternal relations between the two governments and parties. A couple of months later, frightened at the spread of Titoist influence in Eastern Europe, they circulated a letter to all satellite Communist parties warning them against it. In October and November, when Hungary erupted, the Yugoslav regime cheered the fall of the old order, disapproved the first Soviet intervention, hoped that Imre Nagy would succeed in establishing a national Communist regime, and gave him asylum in the Yugoslav embassy when the Soviet Union intervened again, this time with overwhelming force.[7] The Soviet leaders were any-

[7] Nagy's presence, however, proved embarrassing to the Yugoslavs, and they were willing to give him up on receipt of a pledge by the new Kádár government that he would not be seized. He was immediately taken into custody by Soviet or Hungarian officials, incarcerated, and later tried and executed.

thing but appreciative of Yugoslavia's role, or of Tito's detailed defense of it in a public speech.[8] Yugoslavia was pointedly ignored in Khrushchev's attempts, in late 1956 and early 1957, to restore solidarity to the bloc on a new basis of "voluntary" cooperation.

Later in 1957 there came a partial reconciliation. Tito and Khrushchev met in Bucharest and talked about friendship. Yugoslavia then established diplomatic relations with the Ulbricht regime in East Germany, a step which served Soviet interests and did harm to its own, for Bonn reacted by breaking relations with Belgrade. But this entente was of short duration, for it was followed by the gathering of Communist leaders in November which resulted in the Moscow Declaration. Twelve ruling Communist parties subscribed to a statement of doctrine and policy which supposedly was to guide them all. Marshal Tito, scenting what was in the wind, had found himself too ill to go to Moscow. His two lieutenants who did go, Edvard Kardelj and Aleksandar Ranković, did not sign the declaration. One of its paragraphs affirmed that the national independence of each socialist country was reliably guaranteed by "the solidarity and close unity of the socialist countries." Another referred to "the invincible camp of socialist states, headed by the Soviet Union." In its description of the world situation, despite references to peaceful coexistence, it was strictly a cold-war document.

Again, the Yugoslavs were spectacularly on the outside. Their new party program, drawn up at this time, seemed to ensure that they would remain there. In defining for themselves and for the world where they stood, both on the nature of their socialist system and their interpretation of world trends, the leaders of Yugoslav communism took positions that directly challenged Soviet orthodoxy. In a futile conciliatory move they submitted their draft program to the Soviet Communist party, only to be met by a blast from *Pravda* accusing them of revisionism. The Seventh Congress of the League of Communists of Yugoslavia was then held at Ljubljana in April 1958. Ranković made a strong

[8] Speech at Pula, November 11, 1956, *Borba*, November 16, 1956; English translation in Paul E. Zinner, ed., *National Communism and Popular Revolt in Eastern Europe* (New York: Columbia University Press, 1956), pp. 516-541.

and defiant speech, during which the guests representing the Soviet and East European parties walked out (except the Pole, whose demonstration of solidarity with the Yugoslavs was tempered by the general impression that he was asleep). The Congress adopted the new program. And many were saying that Soviet-Yugoslav relations were back where they were in Stalin's day.

Moscow's suspension of $285 million in credits already promised to Yugoslavia reinforced that impression.[9] Tito was again loudly denounced as a renegade. At a Communist party congress in neighboring Bulgaria, Khrushchev called him a "Trojan horse of imperialism." This mood continued through 1960, when once again the leaders of the world's Communist parties gathered in Moscow, this time with no Yugoslav delegation present. There they issued an agreed 81-party Statement of doctrine and policy which condemned, along with the imperialists, "the Yugoslav variety of international opportunism, a variety of modern revisionist 'theories' in concentrated form." With their "anti-Leninist revisionist programme," the Yugoslav Communists had "severed their country from the socialist camp, [and] made it dependent on so-called 'aid' from U.S. and other imperialists . . ." Revisionism was "the main danger" against which the Communist movement must struggle.[10]

The voice was the voice of Khrushchev, but the language was that of Stalin. It was also the language of Mao Tse-tung, and it is that aspect of it which casts doubt on the interpretation of Soviet policy toward Yugoslavia as a return to the days of Stalin and the Cominform. This so-called second break, the period between 1957 and 1960, never went as deep as the first. Diplomatic relations between Yugoslavia and the Soviet Union remained on the ambassadorial level. Major Soviet aid was suspended, but

[9] In 1956, long-term credits were granted to Yugoslavia by the Soviet Union ($110 million) and by East Germany and the Soviet Union jointly ($175 million). They were unilaterally postponed by the Soviet Union in February 1957, reinstated the following July, and postponed again in May 1958. Each move corresponded to a change in the temperature of Soviet-Yugoslav political relations. See George W. Hoffman and Fred Warner Neal, *Yugoslavia and the New Communism* (New York: Twentieth Century Fund, 1962), pp. 342-344.

[10] *New Times*, no. 50, December 1960, Supplement, p. 15.

trade went on. There was no return to full-blown economic warfare. Even the Soviet propaganda, vicious as much of it was, did not approach the depths of vituperation reached in Stalin's time. On the Yugoslav side, the tendency was to tone down the controversy and keep official relations with the Soviet Union and the other Eastern European states as normal as possible.

The Soviet leadership was not trying, as it had before, to overthrow the Tito regime. Khrushchev did not wish to go back on the Belgrade Declaration of 1955. He merely wished to go on interpreting it in his own way. Meanwhile, Soviet-Yugoslav relations had been thrown into a new focus by the dispute with Communist China. After several years of increasingly serious differences, open Soviet-Chinese polemics had broken out at a congress of the Rumanian Communist party in June 1960. The condemnation of Yugoslav revisionism that had appeared in the 81-party Statement of December of that year was stronger, because of Chinese insistence, than the Soviets would have liked.[11] Since early 1958 the Yugoslav "revisionists" had been the target of abusive attacks by the Chinese, which the Soviet leaders could see were indirectly aimed at themselves.

### American Help Follows the Ups and Downs

American attitudes followed the course of Yugoslav-Soviet relations on a comparable fever chart. When the two Communist states were getting on well and talking of solidarity, the United States was worried about aiding its enemies and being taken in. When the Yugoslavs were at odds with Moscow and denounced as incorrigible revisionists, American officials felt reassured and congratulated themselves on their perspicacity. After Tito's visit to the Soviet Union in mid-1956, the United States somewhat

[11] Donald S. Zagoria, *The Sino-Soviet Conflict, 1956-61* (Princeton: Princeton University Press, 1962), pp. 363-364. Khrushchev's authoritative and important speech of January 6, 1961, explaining the Statement to Soviet party workers, said only that "the Communist Parties have unanimously condemned the Yugoslav brand of present-day revisionism." He noted that while revisionism was the chief danger at the moment, dogmatism and sectarianism could become the chief danger if a consistent struggle was not waged against them. See *Current Digest of the Soviet Press*, vol. 13, no. 4 (February 22, 1961), p. 14.

fearfully suspended both economic and military assistance while reviewing its whole policy. In October of the same year, when clouds appeared in the clear sky of Soviet-Yugoslav reconciliation, the President "found" from the available evidence that Yugoslavia remained independent of Soviet control and desired to continue to be independent; economic aid, without which there was "danger that Yugoslavia will be unable to maintain its independence," was then resumed.[12] Military aid, including 200 jet aircraft, went forward again in May 1957, when Soviet-Yugoslav relations were still suffering from the shock of the Hungarian revolt. The reasoning was the same, with the added consideration that Yugoslavia was being put in a disadvantageous position by deliveries of modern Soviet equipment to its Warsaw Pact neighbors.[13]

In the autumn of 1957, when Washington was again worrying about Yugoslavia's independence and asking Tito to give new assurances that he was not going to compromise it, the Yugoslav leader himself took the decision to terminate the whole military aid program. From this time onward, U.S. economic aid shipments largely took the form of surplus agricultural products under Public Law 480, but other kinds of assistance came more easily at times when Belgrade and Moscow were quarreling. In 1959, after the Soviet Union and East Germany suspended their promised credits to Yugoslavia for certain industrial projects, the United States stepped in with credits from the Development Loan Fund (totaling $51.5 million) to help finance some of the projects involved.

The year 1959 was blessed with good growing weather and produced for Yugoslavia a record harvest. The investments in seeds, fertilizers, and improved techniques seemed finally to be paying off. There was much talk of the country's being "over the hump," now able to feed itself and to dispense with outside help. But the cheering was premature. The crops for 1960 were well below those of 1959. Yugoslavia still had an unsolved balance-of-

[12] Paul E. Zinner (ed.), *Documents on American Foreign Relations, 1956* (Harper, for the Council on Foreign Relations, 1957), pp. 268-270.
[13] Paul E. Zinner (ed.), *Documents on American Foreign Relations, 1957* (Harper, for the Council on Foreign Relations, 1958), pp. 193-194.

payments problem after a decade of grants and credits intended to solve it. It was obviously a time for reassessment, economic as well as political, both on the Yugoslav and on the American side.

In order to understand the nature of the choices to be made in the future, as well as to see the economic cost of those made in the past, it is instructive to look at the rough quantities and the general character of American aid in the five-year period from mid-1955 to mid-1960. It gives a measure of the amount of material support for Tito's "neutral" position after his initial reconciliation with Khrushchev, and can be compared with (or added to) the amounts provided to help defend Yugoslavia against Moscow's cold war in the preceding five-year period.[14]

The military aid program, as we noted, came to an end by decisions taken in 1957. Within less than one year the "pipeline" was empty, and no further equipment was sent. The value of military aid—an arbitrary figure at best—is given by official U.S. sources as $105.4 million, from mid-1955 to the ending of deliveries in 1958. For the whole period, from 1951, the official total was $693.9 million.[15] Thereafter, Yugoslavia paid cash for additional equipment and the spare parts that were needed.

The tripartite U.S.-British-French program of economic aid to Yugoslavia had been abandoned even before the Soviet-Yugoslav reconciliation of 1955. The British and the French no longer saw the situation as urgent enough to require continuing grant aid on their part, and the Americans would carry on without them. The Americans did, making funds available each year for general support of the Yugoslav economy from the annual foreign aid appropriation. Under increasing criticism in the Congress, those grants came to an end in 1957. Thereafter, U.S. aid to Yugoslavia took mainly three forms: sales of agricultural surpluses, chiefly wheat, for local Yugoslav currency under Public Law 480; occasional loans through the Development Loan Fund to finance specific projects; and continuation of technical assistance pro-

[14] See page 28, above, and Appendix Table, page 171, below.
[15] International Cooperation Administration, *U.S. Foreign Assistance and Assistance from International Organizations: Obligations and other Commitments,* July 1, 1945 through June 30, 1960, p. 23.

grams, including the training of Yugoslavs in the United States. The figures for the five years from mid-1955 to mid-1960 were still impressive, even though the largest portion was in sales of surplus food, which the U.S. government was happy to dispose of in this way and involved no new burden on the American tax-payer, except the cost of transportation. The rough total was $632.1 million, compared to $598.5 million in the previous five-year period.[16]

Again the familiar question may be asked: Was it worth it? The relationship between American aid and Yugoslavia's inde-pendence was far less clear than in the preceding period. There is no solid justification for saying that Yugoslavia would have gone under without its annual gift from Washington. The argument must be directed, rather, to whether the role played by inde-pendent Yugoslavia, which was basically determined by the Tito regime's own choice, benefited American and Western interests, and whether American aid influenced that role either by encour-aging its beneficial aspects or discouraging alternative and less favorable tendencies.

An element of speculation must enter any retrospective judg-ment, just as it entered into the policy decisions of the time. There is little doubt about the following points: Yugoslavia deliberately limited its rapprochement with Moscow, carefully maintaining its full sovereignty both in internal and external affairs; it definitely exercised a disruptive influence on the Soviet bloc; and it maintained good relations with the West, especially with its immediate neighbors, Austria, Italy, and Greece.

American aid eased Yugoslavia's economic situation and gave its government flexibility in the pursuit of its policies. It is diffi-cult to argue, from the American viewpoint, that the economic price for the policy was prohibitive, or anything more than modest, considering the nature of the military and economic aid to Yugoslavia and the small share of total U.S. foreign aid it represented. On the political side, the policy's value was thrown into question by Yugoslav hostility toward American policy on Germany, NATO, the Middle East, and other important inter-

[16] Of the total, $468.4 million was in aid under PL 480, $136.5 million was in loans, and only $27 million was in direct grant aid.

national questions. But that was one of the attributes of independence. Foreign aid helped Yugoslavia, or rather the Tito regime, to be itself; and being itself included freedom to criticize any other nation, whether the United States, the Soviet Union, or Communist China—and it was critical of all three.

It can be argued, plausibly, that Yugoslavia would have maintained its independence anyway, regardless of American aid, and that it would have opposed the United States on many international questions anyway, regardless of the closeness of its ties with Moscow. In other words, American influence was not in any sense decisive. Yet it was by no means without weight, for the success of Yugoslavia's middle position depended on its ties with *both* great powers. Looked at in a merely negative way, the policies followed by the United States carried a smaller risk of damage to American interests than leaving the Yugoslavs to their own devices. Seen positively, they helped to keep Yugoslavia looking westward as well as eastward.

## Chapter IV

# 1962: The New Rapprochement

Perhaps the most remarkable thing about the Eisenhower-Dulles policy toward Yugoslavia was that, despite all differences in style and language, and in world conditions, it was so similar to that of Truman and Acheson. The United States continued to deal differently with Yugoslavia, compared to other Communist states, placing calculated national interests above its well-advertised distaste for communism. Seeing Yugoslav independence as the main issue, it accepted the risks and annoyances of Tito's return to closer relations with the Soviet bloc and his multifarious diplomatic activity among the neutralist states of Asia and Africa. It continued economic aid, though gradually scaling it down as both the American sense of urgency and the Yugoslav need for help decreased.

As the decade of the 1950s came to an end, a basis seemed to have been established for a relatively normal relationship in which the interests of both countries would be well served. When the Kennedy administration took office in 1961, there was no expectation of a change in the basic policies followed by its predecessors. If anything, the prospect was for a strengthening of ties with Yugoslavia. As a Senator, John Kennedy had consistently supported aid to Yugoslavia. He had also, in 1958 and 1959, proposed giving the President discretion to extend aid to other Communist countries (except the Soviet Union and Communist states in the Far East) whenever he determined that it was important to the security of the United States. The purpose was to enable them to achieve a measure of freedom from Soviet domination and control, or reduce their economic dependence on the Sino-Soviet bloc if they should succeed in gaining greater political independence.[1] During his campaign for the presidency, he had talked of the need for a more active policy in Eastern Europe through trade and cultural exchanges. In his first State of the Union message he referred again to the need for flexibility on aid to Communist countries, having in mind especially Poland. He did not specifically mention Yugoslavia, where active trade and cultural ties already existed, but relations with that country, the first in Communist Eastern Europe to move to independence and normal relations with the West, would continue to set the example.

Ironically, at this very juncture developments on both sides cast darker clouds over Yugoslav-American relations than at any time since 1948, clouds which never really lifted throughout the whole of President Kennedy's period in office. On the one hand, there was a shift in the climate of American opinion toward a doctrinaire anticommunism that enveloped relations with Yugoslavia as well as with Communist states more hostile and more dangerous. On the other, there were signs of more cordial Soviet-Yugoslav relations, with the inevitable result: new doubts and more reappraisals in Washington.

From 1948 onward, a segment of American opinion had opposed, on ideological grounds, aid to Yugoslavia and friendly relations with the Tito regime. The reasoning was that this was a Communist government which had taken power by force, persecuted religion, and denied human rights to its own people; that it was only using our aid for its own ends, which were basically hostile to the United States; that in a showdown it would be with

---

[1] Senator Kennedy first offered this proposal as an amendment to the Mutual Security Act of 1958, though in fact it would amend the Mutual Defense Assistance Control Act (Battle Act). Although the administration supported it in principle—and the Department of State even drafted the precise language—the President cut the ground from under its supporters at the last moment by stating that he did not favor including the provision in this particular legislation. It lost by a 43-42 vote. See *Congressional Record*, vol. 104, Part 8, 85th Cong., 2d sess., June 5, 1958, pp. 10274-10302. In the following year the Senate passed it as an amendment to the Battle Act in September 1959 (by a vote of 49-40, with Kennedy and Goldwater absent and paired) and again in May 1961, but it never was passed by the House.

the Soviets against the West; and that the United States was not acting morally or in its own interest in aiding any Communist regime, whatever its differences with others. Some even maintained that the whole Yugoslav-Soviet controversy was a gigantic hoax.

Many supporters of the above views were convinced of the rightness of their position by Tito's reconciliation with the Soviet Union in 1955. Consequently, as one crisis followed another in Soviet-American relations, they opposed aid to Yugoslavia more than ever as aid to the enemy. Yugoslavia's proclaimed nonalignment did not impress them, for they saw it as a deception. They were generally opposed as well to aiding India, Egypt, Indonesia, and other neutralist states which were at odds with the West on many issues and were cooperating in greater or less degree with the Communist powers. Yugoslav neutralism was even more distasteful because it was the declared policy of a Communist government.

This current of opinion was not strong enough to dictate American policy. Yet it did have considerable support in the Congress, where periodic attempts were made to cut down or cut off the flow of aid to Yugoslavia. Representative Edna Kelly of Brooklyn, though she had voted for the original food relief bill in 1950, thereafter took the lead in such attempts year after year as the House considered the annual foreign aid authorization and related legislation. She never wavered from her position that Yugoslavia should get no aid at all, for "I have greater fear over the new, nationalistic, communist governments like Yugoslavia than I have over the Russian-controlled governments."[2] Senators William Knowland and Frank Lausche played much the same role in the Senate. As Senator Alexander Wiley said to one government witness at the hearings on the first Mutual Security Act specifically including aid to Yugoslavia, "I do not have to tell you that there is a lot of opposition to that aid to Yugoslavia."[3]

[2] *The Mutual Security Program,* Hearings before the Committee on Foreign Affairs, House of Representatives, 82d Cong., 1st sess., July 2, 1951, p. 109.
[3] *Mutual Security Act of 1952,* Hearings before the Committee on Foreign Relations of the U.S. Senate, 82d Cong., 2d sess. (Washington: GPO, 1952), p. 384.

In the later 1950s, hearings and debates on the legislation bore manifold signs of that opposition. In 1955, Mrs. Kelly mustered 52 votes to cut off all aid to Yugoslavia, whereas a similar amendment in 1952 had been defeated without even a vote count. In the following year, the new version of the Mutual Security Act stipulated that all aid to Yugoslavia should be discontinued unless the President should determine that that country remained independent of Soviet control and was not "participating in any policy or program for the Communist conquest of the world," in addition to making his usual finding that it was in the interest of the national security of the United States. The Mutual Security Act of 1957 added that the President should continuously assure himself on those points and report to the Congress. The legislators could not seem to get enough assurances, but they continued to leave to the President the flexibility to decide and to act. After 1957 the opponents of aid were somewhat appeased by the ending of military aid and by the administration's decision not to request further grants for Yugoslavia out of mutual security funds except relatively small amounts for technical cooperation and "special assistance."

In 1960, anti-Communist sentiment fed on the U-2 affair, the fiasco of the summit conference in Paris, and especially the turn toward the Communist powers and the continued intense anti-Americanism displayed by Fidel Castro's regime in Cuba. Then, in 1961, the heating up of the Berlin crisis by Khrushchev and the real possibility of war helped to create an atmosphere of general exasperation against all Communists of whatever variety. In September, the Belgrade Conference of neutralist countries, where President Tito was very free with his criticism of American policies and sympathetic with those of the Soviet Union, made Yugoslavia a special object of public resentment in America.

In this heated atmosphere, an incident in Texas in October almost inevitably produced a flare-up in Congress against the administration's policy. It was suddenly brought to light, by *The Dallas News*, that the United States was supplying jet fighter aircraft to Yugoslavia and that Yugoslav pilots were being trained in Texas to fly them. Senator Tower indignantly declared that the pilots should be shipped home and no planes sent, as "it's foolish to sell arms to the enemy."[4] Such deliveries were in fact no secret matter and were fully in accord with procedures agreed between the United States and Yugoslavia after the termination of the military aid program in 1957, so that the Yugoslavs could obtain, by purchase, planes and spare parts of the types we had previously given them. This particular deal involving 130 obsolescent planes (F-86D Sabrejets) had been concluded in January 1961, a few days before President Eisenhower left office. Aside from being a normal transaction and a logical consequence of the earlier program, it had the merit of keeping Yugoslavia looking to the United States rather than to the Soviet Union for its military equipment. Secretary Rusk defended the arrangement on those grounds, and the planes were in due course delivered. The mood in Congress remained sullen and suspicious.[5]

The incident of the airplanes was of no great intrinsic importance, although apparently the Yugoslav leaders drew the conclusion that they could not count on their agreements with the United States and began to buy arms from the Soviet Union. The barrage of criticism in Congress and the press added to the impression that the United States was waging an ideological war against them in a way it had not done before. A series of incidents sparked by anti-Tito Yugoslav emigrés did not help the situation.

This atmosphere gravely complicated the task of George F. Kennan, whom President Kennedy had sent as Ambassador to Belgrade. The Yugoslavs were pleased by the appointment, because it bore witness to the value the new President put on relations with their country. For the United States government, and for Mr. Kennan himself, it was an attempt to put those relations on a sounder footing of mutual respect and understanding. It placed in Belgrade a man admirably qualified to represent America and interpret its policies, and who at the same time,

[4] *The New York Times*, October 14, 1961.
[5] Although the planes were in fact cash purchases for dollars, for technical legislative reasons the transactions had to be handled through the military aid program, with Yugoslav payments going to the Treasury and deliveries made by the Pentagon, a procedure which may have confused the issue in the minds of some Congressmen.

because of his long experience in dealing with the Soviet Union and matters pertaining to Communist ideology and conduct, gave the United States an expert observer on the scene able to talk to the Yugoslav leaders in their terms and to provide keen analysis and advice to Washington.

With opinion on the American side already touchy and doubtful about Yugoslavia, Ambassador Kennan's quest for a sounder basis for relations was difficult enough. Events on the Yugoslav side, at about the same time, knocked the bottom out of it. September 1, 1961, was the date of the opening of the Belgrade Conference of heads of state and of government representing twenty-five nonaligned countries.[6] This was not a meeting in which the United States took any extraordinary interest, except perhaps as a test of the political realism of the participants. But for the Yugoslavs it was of the utmost importance. It was to put Belgrade on the world map, as leaders from five continents gathered there, and to provide new international prestige for the host country. Just as Bandung in 1955 had signaled the arrival of the new nations of Asia and Africa on the international stage, so Belgrade in 1961 was to speak up for the world of the nonaligned. The authoritative voices would be those of Nehru and Nasser, who had been at Bandung, and especially of Tito himself.

On August 30, as the delegates were gathering in Belgrade, Premier Khrushchev suddenly announced the resumption of Soviet testing of nuclear weapons, thereby breaking the moratorium which the three major nuclear powers (the United States, Great Britain, and the U.S.S.R.) had observed for more than two years. From September 1 onward, the Belgrade meetings were punctuated by explosions of huge and "dirty" nuclear bombs on Soviet territory.

The United States, which had accepted certain risks to its own security by observing the moratorium, in the interest of paving the way to an effective test-ban treaty, took the Soviet violation with utmost seriousness. It did not see how the nonaligned na-

---

[6] All except Yugoslavia, Cyprus, and Cuba were located in Asia or Africa. In addition, three other Latin American countries (Bolivia, Brazil, and Ecuador) were represented by observers.

tions, especially Yugoslavia, could fail to condemn it and maintain any honesty at all, in view of all they had said in the past about American testing. Washington, therefore, paid close attention to President Tito's major speech before the Belgrade Conference on September 3. It was a way of seeing what nonalignment really meant in a clear and concrete case.

In a wide-ranging survey which covered Germany, the Congo, Cuba, colonialism, and the role of the United Nations in a manner generally critical of Western policies though not following the Soviet line on all points, Tito gave special attention to disarmament and nuclear testing. On general disarmament he deplored the fact that no progress had been made, blamed the great powers generally, and especially "the tendency of those who continue to make a fetish of control" (i.e., the United States), showing their "unwillingness or hesitation to undertake real disarmament." He then took cognizance of the Soviet Union's resumption of test explosions, after mentioning that France had already been testing, by stating that it "does not surprise us, because we can understand the reasons the Soviet government has given," though he admitted being more surprised by Moscow's timing in choosing "the day of the opening of this conference of peace." It was necessary, therefore, to resume negotiations.[7]

This was putting the Soviet Union and the United States on the same plane, though one had kept the moratorium and the other had broken it. More than that, Tito's expressed "understanding" of the Soviet action seemed an explicit acceptance of the Kremlin's explanation of its decision. Washington was naturally indignant. Ambassador Kennan, especially, felt a per-

[7] Original text in *Borba*, September 4, 1961. After the sharp American reaction to Tito's statements, it was said by some officials in Belgrade that the Western press had exaggerated or misinterpreted him. Actually, the offensive sentence was inserted in the distributed mimeographed copies of the speech on a separate slip of paper, apparently the result of a last-minute decision taken by Tito after some hurried conferences with the Soviet Ambassador. The English language version published in book form after the conference omits the two sentences referring to Tito's understanding of Soviet reasoning and his surprise about the timing. See *The Conference of Heads of State or Government of Non-Aligned Countries,* (Belgrade: Jugoslavija, 1961), p. 156.

sonal disillusionment with Tito, who in an instant had torn down all that the Ambassador thought he had been building up. The foreign press in Belgrade was aware of this reaction and pulled no punches in writing about it. The U.S. government showed its annoyance by putting off consideration of Yugoslavia's current request for aid in surplus food products. Yugoslav-American relations were at a new low point.

In retrospect, it may be said that neither side was helpful even to its own interests in this affair. Tito was inexcusably crude or careless in his choice of language. He went far beyond what his State Secretary for Foreign Affairs, Koča Popović, had said in a statement to the press on September 1 regretting the Soviet government's decision.[8] It can be explained, in addition to direct Soviet influence, by his concentration on making a success of the Belgrade Conference. The whole purpose of the conference, in the view of the Yugoslav hosts, was a ringing reaffirmation of nonalignment and the search for peace. Such a variety of countries and leaders was represented—from Sukarno to Bourguiba—that it was risky to depart from vague generalities, and especially to introduce a condemnation of one side in the cold war on any concrete issue (except, of course, colonialism). Tito therefore shied away from any denunciation of the Soviets, either as a proposal for the conference or a specific statement of Yugoslavia's position.

Marshal Tito's failure to take a stand, moreover, was not really out of line with what Yugoslavia had done in the past on such matters as nuclear testing, arms control, and disarmament. It had always encouraged moving ahead from current positions, whatever they were, toward future agreement. Because the Soviet Union frequently called for general agreements to ban nuclear weapons and to disarm without further ado, while the United States kept insisting on inspection and enforcement, the Yugoslav government had rather consistently leaned more to the Soviet than to the Western side. While Tito probably underestimated the American reaction in this instance, evidently he either did not bother to think about it before making his remarks, or did in fact anticipate and discount it in advance.

[8] *Borba,* September 2, 1961.

On the American side, exasperation with the Soviets for their action seems to have flowed over into relations with the neutrals. Because the matter of a nuclear test ban was so crucial, the American reaction to a neutralism that was "neutral in favor of the other side" was more colored with moral indignation than on comparable occasions in the past. Tito's remarks should not have been quite so unexpected; although the international forum was of a different order of importance than the setting of other speeches, Yugoslav officials had been making statements unfavorable to America for some years. Indignation may well have been indicated, but it might have been kept in a lower key.

The incident was unfortunate in that it was peripheral to the basic interests tied up in the Yugoslav-American relationship. It was not vital to the United States that Yugoslavia should accept the American positions on nuclear testing and disarmament, or that it should denounce the Soviet Union even in such a clear case as this. Nor was it vital to Yugoslavia that its president should give this further demonstration of a "double standard" in dealing with the East and the West. The success of his conference did not depend on it; Abdel Nasser and Nehru both took a more moderate position. The net result was that the ill feeling engendered on both sides affected the whole relationship, and in that way had a baneful influence on matters that were more important.

During the following months, under the sting of Tito's remarks, the Executive Branch of the U.S. government made its own contribution to the anti-Yugoslav feeling already evident in the legislature. The Congress, thereafter, was even more inclined to bear down heavily on Yugoslavia in legislation affecting trade and aid, and also to take away from the executive the flexibility it had previously had in dealing with Yugoslavia on those matters. In the next few years the President, the Department of State, and the U.S. Ambassador to Yugoslavia found themselves battling to keep that flexibility, and not with uniform success. Kennan's efforts to put Yugoslav-American relations on a normal working basis that would best serve our political objectives ran into such opposition and disregard of his advice on the part of Congress that, although he did indeed do a great deal for the improvement of relations, he ultimately came to the conclusion that he could not achieve anything of major constructive significance in Belgrade. He resigned his post in 1963.

### The Economic Tests of Policy

The basic factors in Yugoslav-American relations, as in Yugoslavia's relations with East and West generally, were and are political. As we have seen, however, the concrete questions for decision on both sides frequently have been economic. In the early 1960s it is in the economic issues and decisions that we can best follow the story.

The Yugoslav economy had grown remarkably in the 1950s, partly through the same kind of rapid and forced industrialization that took place in other countries of Eastern Europe, partly through a series of reforms which had made it less centralized and more open. Yet there were still some fundamental weaknesses: a backward agriculture, uneconomic industries, inflation, and a persistent deficit in the international balance of payments. Those weaknesses had been covered up to some extent by the considerable volume of foreign aid; but in spite of that help, Yugoslavia in 1960 entered a period of uncertainty in which revaluation of the currency and additional outside assistance were needed to stabilize the economy for a renewed advance. Thus, in the following year the government carried through a major financial reform, made possible by funds from the United States, certain European nations, and the International Monetary Fund. The anticipated result was a sounder basis for production and for foreign trade.

In actuality, the reform and the outside assistance were too limited to bring about that result. The economy's rate of growth began to decline. Agricultural production could not get back to the relatively high level of 1959. The investment system was not working well, consumption continued to outrun production, the deficit in the international balance of payments was not reduced, and the burden of debt service was growing ever heavier. By early 1962, the signs of an economic crisis were present. At this juncture President Tito in a major speech called for drastic action to check the adverse trends and spoke of the need for greater party discipline, awakening fears of a return to more dictatorial and centralized means of control.[9] There was no decision, however, to move sharply either forward to greater liberalism or backward to strict central control, and there was no purge. The ensuing measures made some changes in the administrative structure and reshuffled the major economic officials, but did not attack the real problems. In Yugoslavia, it has been said, when the orchestra plays badly, the musicians are not fired; they merely exchange instruments.

Meanwhile, the Yugoslavs saw their international position growing more troublesome. Difficulties in trade with the United States and with Western Europe, where Yugoslavia's main trading partners were in the increasingly exclusive European Economic Community, led many officials to think more seriously of a major turn to the East for trade and economic cooperation. Here the whole subject of economic policy and of the directions of trade took on political overtones.

There was no clear-cut drawing of lines, but the choices facing the country inevitably created divisions within it. The differences between the "liberals" and the "centralists" grew sharper. Those in the former group, moreover, tended to look to the West and to participation in the economic relations of the non-Communist world, while the latter favored broadening and strengthening the ties with the Soviet Union and Eastern Europe. To make the divergence politically more ominous, the major support for liberalism and a Western orientation came from the more advanced parts of the country, especially Slovenia and Croatia, while the other side found backing in traditionally centralist Serbia, in the less developed regions which the government had favored economically for political reasons, and among the more entrenched elements of the party apparatus.

At this time the Soviet Union began to make friendly gestures toward Yugoslavia. Relations had been strained by the great campaign against revisionism proclaimed by the Moscow conferences of 1957 and 1960. But by 1960 the Soviet-Chinese dispute was already raging in the open and came to an even sharper

---

[9] Address at Split, May 6, 1962, *Borba*, May 7, 1962.

point in 1961 at the Twenty-second Congress of the Soviet Communist party, where Khrushchev tried to make his case against Albania a test of loyalty to communism, and Chou En-lai responded by walking out. These developments apparently pushed the Soviet leadership to the decision to repair the wire to Belgrade. As Yugoslavia was hardly comparable in size and weight to China as a partner, the decision showed that Khrushchev, at least, must have regarded the break with the Chinese as unbridgeable. The Soviet leaders may also have felt that Yugoslavia could be brought in as a stabilizing factor in the relations between the Soviet Union and some of its restless East European allies, which were not above exploiting the Soviet-Chinese dispute for their own ends. They may well have seen a danger of isolation, especially if both Chinese and Yugoslav influence were working against the Soviet Union in the Communist world and among the nonaligned.

Premier Khrushchev's speech in the Bulgarian city of Varna in 1962 opened the door. He virtually ordered Bulgaria and Rumania to make up with Tito. Then Leonid Brezhnev, the titular head of the Soviet state, paid a formal visit to Yugoslavia in September. Finally, President Tito went to Moscow in December, his first visit since 1956. This was an extraordinary occasion. Tito, the symbol of revisionism, made a formal address to the Supreme Soviet. Khrushchev spoke also, upholding Yugoslavia's right to be called a socialist state, which had been challenged by "some people." He mentioned that certain ideological differences still remained between the Soviet and Yugoslav parties, but they were no bar to fraternal collaboration on both the governmental and the party level. The Soviet Union was ready, specifically, for more and closer economic cooperation.

Tito was undoubtedly impressed by his welcome, by the prospects of cooperation, and above all by the magnitude of his own political triumph. He had achieved, by following an independent line, what others had failed to achieve through humble obedience. He had no hesitation in responding to the Soviet overtures; and he did not see his stake in relations with the West as so great that it could not be put to this test. Nevertheless, he maintained his reservations, as he had in 1955 and 1957. He stated, when he got home, that there would be no basic change in Yugoslavia's policy. It wished to keep its relations with the West, as with all nations, on a normal and friendly basis. However, a definite change in the temperature of relations with the East had occurred, to which a number of concrete economic agreements bore witness. Economically, Yugoslavia was becoming a kind of associate of the Soviet bloc, though without giving up one bit of its independence. It concluded new trade treaties and agreements for technical cooperation with several East European states. It expressed a desire to have observer status in the Council for Mutual Economic Assistance (CMEA), and in due course (in 1965) was invited to participate in certain of its commissions. On the political side, Yugoslav speeches and statements were filled with many more references to the "international workers' movement" and Yugoslavia's part in it. Both in foreign and in domestic policies there was a perceptible narrowing of the gap between Soviet and Yugoslav positions.

This rapprochement, however, by no means solved Yugoslavia's economic problems. There was no certainty or even very high expectation that the Yugoslavs could really get from the Soviet Union or Eastern Europe the credits and the kinds of goods they needed. Although trade increased somewhat, it did not reach one-third of Yugoslavia's total foreign trade until 1965, and Yugoslav experts do not expect it to go higher.[10] The East was no real or long-term substitute for the West in that regard. Yet the very political gestures that Tito had made toward the East were bound to add to the difficulty in getting a hearing for his case in the West. They added to the ill will or indifference toward Yugoslavia that already existed there, especially in the Congress of the United States.

### Trade and Aid in the U.S. Congress

In this period (1962-64) the Congress played a much more active and influential part in determining American policy to-

[10] In 1963, exports to Eastern Europe (including the U.S.S.R.) were 27 per cent; imports, 23 per cent. In 1964 the respective figures were 35 per cent and 29 per cent. See *Jugoslovenski Pregled*, April 1965, p. 141. In 1965, they were 42 per cent and 29 per cent. See *Indeks*, Belgrade, February 1966, p. 32.

ward Yugoslavia than ever before. The President and the State Department were as little pleased about the Tito regime's moves toward the East as were the members of Congress, but they differed on what to do about it. The Executive Branch wished to retain for the United States the ability to exert influence on the situation, in particular by keeping Western alternatives open to Tito, instead of cutting them off. It regarded trade and aid as useful and necessary instruments to encourage Yugoslavia in following independent policies, especially at a time when other East European states, notably Rumania, were showing signs of independence. The State Department was not convinced that, because Tito had been warmly received in Moscow and had welcomed Khrushchev to Belgrade, the West should forget about Yugoslavia or close off the channels to it.

Presidents Kennedy and Johnson had adherents in the Congress who supported that line of thinking. They also had the power of the presidential office and of their leadership of the Democratic party to influence Congressmen in the desired direction. It was a measure of how indifferent or adverse the majority in Congress was that both House and Senate so often went their own way on Yugoslav matters or followed the President only reluctantly. Many Congressmen simply took the view that aid to Yugoslavia did not serve American interests and looked upon specific legislation as the only way to prevent the administration from going ahead with it. Others who supported the President's argument for the power to act or not to act, as the national interest in his judgment demanded, were also in favor of providing nothing to Yugoslavia at that particular time.

Much of the congressional animus against aid to Yugoslavia, however, was merely part of a general dissatisfaction with the entire foreign aid program. It was becoming harder each year to persuade the legislators to appropriate as much money for the program as the administration thought essential, or to provide anything at all for countries whose current policies or official statements seemed to be antagonistic to the United States and its interests. The United Arab Republic and Indonesia were prominent in this category, as were the two Communist states receiving aid, Poland and Yugoslavia; the latter two could be hit in the field of trade policy as well.

To illustrate the case of Yugoslavia, it is enough to give the bare bones of the story. The Senate, in June 1962, adopted amendments to the administration's aid bill which would have banned all aid to any country known to be dominated by communism or Marxism, except surplus agricultural products which could still be sold for local currency under Public Law 480.[11] After strong administration pressure and much argument on both the authorization and appropriation bills, the final result was a sweeping prohibition on all aid to Communist countries, with the customary saving clause that the restriction could be waived only if the President made the necessary findings that the aid was "vital" to American security and would promote the independence of the recipient country from international communism, and that that country was in fact not controlled by the "international Communist conspiracy." The President would have no difficulty about the last two points, but it was not so easy to justify as "vital" a policy better described as sensible and reasonable.

As a crowning blow, the Congress, in the Trade Expansion Act of 1962, directed the President to withdraw, "as soon as practicable," application of existing or future tariff treatment to products "of any country or area dominated or controlled by Communism." The President was thus obligated to give notice of termination of the existing Treaty of Commerce and Navigation with Yugoslavia, so that within a year from that notice Yugoslav imports to the United States would lose the benefit of most-favored-nation treatment. This was a treaty dating from 1881 which had never been challenged; even in the period of Yugoslavia's loyalty to Stalin the United States had accorded most-favored-nation treatment.

Termination of the treaty would have dealt a body blow to Yugoslavia's trade with the United States and to its chances of coping with its balance-of-payments deficit. President Kennedy had to accept the provision, although it had been passed over his

[11] The passage of the original amendment, banning all aid including PL 480, by a 57-24 vote was an indication of the strength of anti-Yugoslav sentiment. On the next day, a new amendment sponsored by the leadership of both parties excepted PL 480 aid from the ban. See *Congressional Record*, vol. 108, Part 7, 87th Cong., 2d sess., June 6, 7, 1962, pp. 9862-9871, 9916-9932.

known opposition, because the Trade Expansion Act as a whole was too important to veto. The administration gave a liberal interpretation of the reasonable time permitted before giving notice of intention to terminate the treaty, meanwhile announcing its intention to try to persuade Congress to reverse itself. This time the White House and the State Department really worked hard and with ultimate success. The Foreign Assistance Act of 1963, passed shortly after President Kennedy's death, amended the earlier provision of the Trade Expansion Act and thus made it possible to keep the most-favored-nation clause in force for Yugoslavia and Poland.

The Yugoslav government, well informed by its able representatives in Washington, was not indifferent to the administration's troubles with the Congress. Beyond letting it be known that loss of most-favored-nation treatment in trade would be a blow from which relations between the two nations could not easily recover, Yugoslav officials kept their counsel and were "correct" in their mien. They took the line that their general principles of policy would not change. They would continue to seek good relations with the West and increased trade with other Western countries even if rebuffed by the United States. It was apparent that they did not want to see the end of good working relations with the United States, not just because they valued the aid and the export market in themselves but because these were part of a line to the West as important for Yugoslavia's international position as for its economic future. There was a common interest, almost swept aside by the arguments and mishaps of the past few years, that both sides wished to preserve.

The time was deemed ripe in 1963 for the President to invite Marshal Tito to Washington. Such a visit was long overdue. It had first been talked of in the early 1950s but never received high-level approval. In 1957, after an informal agreement with the Yugoslav Goverment had already been made, heated protests by various Yugoslav-American and other groups and by a number of members of Congress caused President Eisenhower and Secretary Dulles to back away. After Khrushchev's visit in 1959 it hardly made sense to keep Tito in the "untouchable" category. President Eisenhower met him in New York during the U.N. session of 1960, but the atmosphere in Yugoslav-American relations was not sufficiently calm for a visit to Washington until three years later.

The character of the visit, which took place in October 1963, reflected the fact that this was no normal call from a friendly head of state. There was no triumphal ride by the two presidents through cheering crowds—in fact, no public appearance at all. Tito got the 21-gun salute to which he was entitled by protocol on arrival at Andrews Air Force Base, then a helicopter deposited him on the White House lawn. President Kennedy chose not to test his guest's popularity with the local citizenry.

The conversations went well. The two presidents apparently hit it off—but there was nothing vital to negotiate. The official communiqué noted that direct American assistance to Yugoslavia was no longer needed. The significance of the meeting lay in the fact that it took place. The symbol of independent communism, who had had his great moments of triumph in Moscow and had been to London to visit the Queen, not to speak of meetings with dozens of other heads of state, had finally been received by the President of the United States. But the contrast between those other visits and the almost surreptitious character of the Washington meeting could hardly be overlooked.

The few days in New York, featuring an address to the United Nations but marked also by minor street demonstrations, an abortive reception cancelled on "security" grounds, and the success of a Croatian emigré with unfriendly intent in reaching the corridor outside Tito's suite in the Waldorf-Astoria, provided a nightmarish sequel. On leaving for home the Yugoslav President sent a polite farewell message to Kennedy, stating his conviction that their talks would lead to further cooperation between the two countries. But the whole affair had shown that the relationship with Communist Yugoslavia, for the American public anyway, was shadowed by questioning and doubt, in addition to some outright hostility.

American opinion, of course, should not be equated with the feelings of those who made the most noise on the streets, many of whom were of Yugoslav origin and may have had quite understandable personal or political reasons for disliking Tito and his regime. Yet the American people certainly did not rush forward to cheer and welcome Tito as the head of a friendly state. While the public instinct may have been sound on that point, a general popular attitude should not necessarily be the determining factor in the U.S. government's policy toward any country. But public emotions and attitudes are political facts, which can limit policy or help it. The government should have been the first to admit that it had not really succeeded in explaining its Yugoslav policy to the American public. And the Executive Branch had succeeded less and less, in recent years, in convincing the Congress to support it.

There was no perceptible softening in congressional attitudes on aid after Tito's visit, although the decision to withdraw most-favored-nation treatment was reversed. In the following year the act renewing Public Law 480 forbade sales of surplus farm products to Yugoslavia for local currency. Henceforward, purchases would have to be made in dollars. It could be done on credit, under fairly easy terms, but it would remain a dollar obligation and thus in the long run a burden on the balance of payments. The administration, by this time tired of fighting with Congress over Yugoslavia on one point after another, accepted the provision without a struggle. But that was not all. The Food for Peace Act, passed by the Congress in October 1966, contained a provision forbidding even dollar credits to any state sending supplies to North Vietnam (Yugoslavia was sending some medicines through the Red Cross) or, with the exception of certain types of goods, to Cuba (there was a trickle of Yugoslav trade). President Johnson spoke out against this restriction on the conduct of foreign policy, but signed the bill.

It is of particular importance that the American people should comprehend Yugoslavia's situation, and the extent of our interest in it, as best these can be determined; that they should see it not in simple ideological terms but as part of a complex pattern involving America's relations with the Soviet Union, Eastern Europe, China, the third world, and the West. The lesson of the past five years is that this minimum basis of understanding is necessary if the government is to be able to carry out a policy in consonance with American interests.

Whether the government will find the right policies is another question. One way to inquire into it is to examine past and current policies in the light of recent conditions and trends. Accordingly, the remaining chapters of this book investigate Yugoslavia's present position and the directions of its internal and external policies as they affect the United States and the interests of the West, and then put forward some conclusions and suggestions for the future.

## Chapter V

# Yugoslavia and the Third World

For a time after they parted company with Moscow in 1948, the Yugoslav Communists still looked on all of world politics, and on their own domestic politics, through the prism of that relationship. And so did others look upon them. Later, when they felt surer of their independence, they began to chart the "Yugoslav way": in their party doctrines, political and economic institutions, attitudes toward other states of Eastern Europe, and policies in the non-Communist world. They began to define and develop their relations with the West, not merely for support against Moscow but in the light of their own plans for economic development and for an independent role. They found a new interest in the United Nations and in what they could do there. They discovered the "third world" of the nonaligned and made Yugoslavia a part of it. In short, Yugoslavia became an active participant in world affairs on its own and in a variety of roles.

Nowhere is this proposition more evident than in Yugoslavia's cult of nonalignment, or neutralism, and solidarity with the new or underdeveloped nations. In 1954 Tito advertised it to the world when he undertook a journey to India and Burma, stopping briefly in Egypt on the way home. In 1955 he hailed the results of the Asian-African Conference at Bandung, declaring that the conceptions dominating the meeting were "fully in accord with our conceptions." In the following year he visited Abdel Nasser in Cairo, and then both Nasser and Nehru met with Tito on the island of Brioni in the Adriatic. Thereafter the comings and goings were thick and fast. Tito went again to Asia and to Africa. A succession of luminaries, from Abboud of Sudan to Sukarno of Indonesia, visited Yugoslavia. Communiqués stressing common devotion to peace and the virtues of nonalignment regularly followed each meeting. Then, with the Belgrade summit conference of 1961, the community of the nonaligned took on a slightly more organized form. An economic conference at Cairo followed in 1962, and then a "second Belgrade," also at Cairo, in 1964.

Throughout all of this activity, Yugoslav officials asserted that they had no intention of forming any kind of third-force bloc. They were, they said, promoting mutual consultation and solidarity among states guided by the concept of nonalignment. Presumably, each could serve itself, its partners, and the world by recognizing and stressing their common interests. Behind the barrage of talk about solidarity and peace and about the evils of alliances and of colonialism, however, each had its own national purposes, interests and policies, none more than Yugoslavia.

We now have had the record of more than a decade of non-alignment as practised by the Yugoslav government. If we are to evaluate this rather extraordinary venture on the part of a small European country, it is less enlightening to follow the conferences and the communiqués than to try to see what Tito and his colleagues were trying to accomplish: what is reality and what is talk; how neutralism, as the basis for an active diplomacy from Southeast Asia to the Congo to Cuba, fits into a foreign policy concerned also with developments nearer home; and above all, how it affects relations with the major Communist powers and with the West.

At the start, it is necessary to distinguish between two main elements in Yugoslav neutralism, which, though related, are separate in their origins. The first is simply the taking of an independent position between East and West, a policy which grew out of the break with the Soviet bloc and the subsequent decisions not to let cooperation with the West become an alliance and to restore "normal" relations with the East when possible. The second element is the conviction that Yugoslavia must be an active and vocal enemy of alliances and blocs, not just a state which refrains from taking part in them. Hence, neutralism had to be a "positive," not a mere passive neutrality like that of Austria or Switzerland.

Tito's reaching out to Asia and Africa to join hands with other neutralists was originally an effort to bolster Yugoslavia's position in Europe. His had not been a comfortable situation trying to keep a balance between fear of the East and suspicion of the West, when a miscalculation in dealing with either side might compromise the regime's independence or threaten its existence. It was better to have some friends, even if they had but little power to throw into the world balance. After 1948 the Yugoslav leaders began to attach some importance to world opinion. In 1951 they took the trouble to work for the adoption by the U.N. General Assembly (a body which before 1948 they had regarded as an instrument of world capitalism) of a resolution reflecting their views and aims in the dispute with the Soviet Union and its satellites. At the United Nations, as elsewhere, they saw advantages in the political and diplomatic influence of the growing number of new nations pleading the cause of independence from the great powers.

India, Egypt, and Yugoslavia, which were in the forefront of the movement, all came to neutralism by different routes corresponding to their national interests and to the character and the style of their leaders: Nehru as the great mediator, the moral force for peace; Nasser as the fiery foe of colonialism and champion of the right of the Arabs to a place in the sun; Tito as the bold defender of national independence between the pressures of two mighty blocs. Other nonaligned states had other motives; some leaned toward cooperation with the West, others in the opposite direction. There is, indeed, no accepted neutralist ideology other than the principle of national self-determination and independence and the absence of military alliances. Anticolonialism was a common ingredient, since so many of the new states were only recently dependencies of Western powers, and their leaders were conditioned by the struggle for freedom. To these guiding ideas may be added the general assumption that the nonaligned, because of their abstention from the cold war, could see world problems more objectively than the committed and thus could make a positive contribution to the cause of peace.

Yugoslavia, like the other more voluble neutralist states, has done its share of preaching the virtues of peace and coexistence, and offering to the great powers gratuitous advice and appeals to compromise their differences. It has also thrown itself into the anticolonial campaign both in propaganda and in active diplomacy, sometimes in apparent willingness to jeopardize its ties with the West for causes hardly vital to its own national interests. For Yugoslavia's leaders, who are a singularly hard-headed group, the "new nations" seemed to have an almost romantic allure. Its economists and political writers, moreover, appear obsessed by the subject of the advancement of those countries and the obligation of the rich nations to do something about it.

Yugoslavs found satisfaction in being not just a small nation but part of a great movement representing half the population of the world, at first perhaps as a substitute for the "socialist world" which had rejected them. The part played by President Tito, whether as mediator or advocate, has been out of all proportion to the size and resources of his country; the contrast with prewar Yugoslavia, or with any other Eastern European country today, is almost breathtaking. But the question remains: How have the ties with Asia and Africa, the summit conferences, the multiplicity of visits, missions and exchanges, served definable Yugoslav interests?

### Trade and Aid

In trading both with the East and with the West, Yugoslavia found itself at a certain disadvantage. Being a country in the intermediate stage of economic development, it needed to import both raw materials for existing industries and capital equipment for further growth. It had to have export markets, but its goods had difficulty overcoming competition in the West, whence needed imports came; in the East it was at first barred from trade altogether by the boycott, and could earn no hard currency when trade was restored. The uncertainties of the situation led the

Yugoslav government to explore a new field of economic relations on other continents, where some answers to pressing problems might be found.

Asia, Africa, and Latin America might provide new markets. Here too, perhaps, were prospects for trade which would give Yugoslavia more bargaining power, and greater insurance against risk, in its economic relations with East and West. As a nonaligned state in the cold war, Yugoslavia might also expect a better political atmosphere for trade relations with the states of the third world than could members of the major blocs. The decision taken, Yugoslav trade delegations and technical aid missions began to turn up in Djakarta, New Delhi, Damascus, Addis Ababa, and a succession of African capitals as little known to Yugoslavs as Belgrade was known there.

The first experiences in the early 1950s were disappointing; political sympathies could not produce fruitful economic exchanges when the right goods were not available at the right prices. In order to establish trading relationships with a number of African states and keep the volume up to the planned level, Yugoslavia sometimes had to accept quantities of bananas, cacao, and other goods for which its need was limited. Trade gradually increased in the first few years, as Yugoslavia demonstrated that it could sell some of its industrial products in the third world in competition with countries of both Eastern and Western blocs. It could provide capital equipment and engineering services needed by underdeveloped countries and by those on more or less the same plane of development as itself.[1] Where the results were disappointing were in the evident limits on the volume of this trade, which leveled off after the initial rise and never reached as much as 18 per cent of Yugoslav exports (except in one year, 1962) or 15 per cent of imports.[2] The fact was that for the most part the countries of the third world could provide neither the capital goods Yugoslavia wanted nor the free cur-

[1] "Cooperation in Investment Projects of Developing Countries," *Yugoslav Survey*, vol. V, no. 18 (July-September, 1964), pp. 2625-2640.

[2] International Monetary Fund and International Bank for Reconstruction and Development, *Direction of Trade, Annual, 1958-62*, pp. 178-179; and same, *1960-64*, pp. 391-392; Milan Aleksić, "Tendencije u razvoju spoljne trgovine Jugoslavije," *Medjunarodni Problemi*, no. 2, 1965, p. 44.

rencies with which these goods could be purchased elsewhere.

Aside from trade, the Yugoslav leaders have taken a special interest in their program of aid to underdeveloped nations. This might seem a strange role for a country which was itself receiving substantial amounts of foreign aid. Actually, unless commercial credits at 3 per cent over seven years, the usual arrangement, be considered as aid, it has been strictly a program of training and technical cooperation tied largely to the export of Yugoslav equipment. No expenditure of hard currency is involved. In any given year after 1955, several thousand Yugoslav engineers and technicians have been made available to other countries for planning and installation of various projects. They have been active in geological exploration, land reclamation, and the designing of industrial projects. Yugoslav firms have built power stations, port installations, shipyards, and industrial plants in dozens of countries from Indonesia to Argentina. The leading partners have been India, Pakistan, Ethiopia, the U.A.R., and Algeria. By providing training in Yugoslavia to students from these countries, mostly in the sciences and in technology, Belgrade has made yet another contribution to their economic development.

It is difficult if not impossible to assign a value in money to the totality of the Yugoslav aid program. It is equally difficult to estimate what it has been worth, tangibly and intangibly, to the recipients and to Yugoslavia. Primarily, the advantages sought and the advantages gained were political. What the Yugoslav economy, in its straitened circumstances, has been able to offer Asian and African nations in trade and aid could be no more than a fractional answer to their basic needs for investment capital and for stable markets, just as it could bring only limited gains to Yugoslavia, which had the same basic needs. But to deal with Yugoslavia had a special attraction for them. First, it was a small country. They did not have to worry about being dominated and exploited. Second, it was a nonaligned country, sharing their own desire to keep out of the cold war (except to profit by it). Third, it was a socialist country, whose independent and experimental brand of socialism found many admirers among their leaders. Yugoslavia stood as living proof that it was possible to be socialist without being dependent on the Soviet Union or China.

As things worked out, many of those countries gained real though minor economic benefits from their trade and aid relations with Yugoslavia, the net result of which was to strengthen pro-Yugoslav political inclinations. Sometimes Yugoslavia was able to provide them with equipment that was cheaper and better suited to their own conditions than what they could get from the advanced industrial countries, and Yugoslav engineers proved to be competent and well trained as well as relatively disinterested, in addition to being less expensive than Western Europeans or Americans. In return, the economic benefit to Yugoslavia was modest, but this manifold activity did add to its credentials for a kind of informal leadership, shared with others, of the underdeveloped and the unaligned.

For the Western nations, Yugoslavia's policies and activities in Asia, Africa, and Latin America raise some important questions. They need not be unduly concerned about the economic effects of Yugoslav trade and aid nor about Yugoslavia's advocacy of the right of underdeveloped nations to more outside help than they have been getting. They have recognized the magnitude of the latter problem and have done something, albeit not enough, to meet it. The important questions, which have to be discussed together, are two: first, whether Yugoslav support for the aims and policies of those countries is injurious to Western interests; and second, whether Yugoslavia has acted in the third world, consciously or unconsciously, as a stalking-horse or partner of the Soviet Union.

### Belgrade's Voice Against the West

To officials in Washington it was disconcerting, even when no longer novel, to have a government which was receiving American aid line up time after time against the United States on international issues both major and minor. For the donor country such a situation requires making a sharp distinction between the considerations of policy which lie behind the provision of aid—such as steady economic development, avoidance of crisis, continuing cooperation—and those other elements in the relations with the recipient on which differences of view exist and mutual criticism is inevitable. It requires also a calculation whether the advantages accruing on the one side outweigh the damage done on the other. Such distinctions and calculations are not easy to make, especially under the pressure of critics on the home front who argue that leaders and nations not with us right down the line have no claim on us for support.

The United States has had to confront many of these situations, since neutralist states like India, Indonesia, or the United Arab Republic, to which it has furnished aid with the purpose of strengthening their independence or maintaining a degree of influence, have been extremely critical of various American policies and at one time or another have given their neutralism an unmistakable anti-Western slant. Yugoslavia, being both neutralist and Communist, has been perhaps the most difficult case of all. Leaving aside the question of aid, let us look at the pattern of Yugoslavia's hostility and at its effects.

The United States has become used to general Yugoslav statements cheering on the peoples struggling against colonialism. They are no cause for protest or undue concern. American public statements have had much the same theme when the talk is in generalities rather than specifics. It is less easy to be tolerant when the United States itself is accused of propping up colonial rule or establishing neocolonialism. Nor was it especially helpful when Tito, after a meeting with Nkrumah or Nasser or Sukarno, would sign a communiqué condemning the "Western imperialists" and saying, with a fine impartiality, that they must get out of all remaining colonies. As the United States was generally trying to push the European colonial powers toward an orderly transfer of power, at a pace somewhat faster than they wished to go, Yugoslavia's moral judgments and attacks struck Washington as irresponsible. Still, the Asian and African nations were saying the same thing on all possible occasions, and the addition to Yugoslavia's voice to the anticolonial chorus made no great difference.

As with speeches, so with conduct in the United Nations. No mere tabulation of votes on specific resolutions can tell the full story, but a sampling of the record on a number of issues concerning Asia and Africa that came before the General Assembly should give an idea of Yugoslavia's general position. The pattern was frequently the same. The Soviet Union would come forward with a strongly worded resolution against colonialism. A group of African and Asian states, unwilling to accept Soviet leadership on issues primarily their own, would present their own less sweeping draft, hoping for a large majority. Yugoslavia would support the Afro-Asian position. Eventually, the Soviet delegation would withdraw its resolution rather than see it voted down. This was what happened in 1960 on the declaration on the early independence of all colonies, when the original Soviet draft was introduced by Nikita Khrushchev himself. It happened again in 1961 on the resolution establishing a Special Committee on Colonialism.[3] The Yugoslav delegates' aspersions on Western policy were hardly relished by the United States, but it was some compensation that they showed themselves as unwilling to follow the leadership of the Soviet Union as to be held back by the restraining hand of the West. Often the final voting showed Yugoslavia, the Soviet Union and the United States all voting with the Afro-Asian group in favor of an anticolonial resolution.[4]

On four draft resolutions on the Congo affair, covering withdrawal of Belgian troops, the character of the Congolese government, and other matters,[5] Yugoslavia voted twice with the Soviet Union and twice in a different way, but always with the Afro-Asian bloc. On Angola, Yugoslavia supported a resolution sponsored by 36 Asian and African members in the General Assembly in April 1961, calling upon Portugal to introduce reforms looking to self-determination, for which the United States and the Soviet Union also voted. The pattern was the same on a similar resolution early in 1962, but different when the Assembly later went so far as to request the Security Council to take sanctions against Portugal.[6] During the debate in January 1962 the Yugoslav delegate described his government's position as "the

[3] Resolutions 1514 (XV), December 14, 1960, and 1654 (XVI), November 27, 1961.

[4] This was true both of the establishment of the Special Committee on Colonialism and of the resolution on its first report (Resolution 1810, XVII, December 17, 1962).

[5] Resolutions 1474 (ES-IV), September 20, 1960; 1599 (XV), 1600 (XV), 1601 (XV), April 15, 1961.

[6] Resolutions 1603 (XV) April 20, 1961; 1742 (XVI) January 30, 1962; 1819 (XVII) December 18, 1962.

same as that adopted by the countries which participated in the Belgrade Conference."[7]

Marshal Tito, however, did not follow his friend Sukarno into the latter's extreme positions against Malaysia and against the United Nations. When delegates of the recently formed Federation of Malaysia (which came into being through the merger of Malaya, Singapore, North Borneo and Sarawak) arrived to occupy the former Malayan seat at the 1963 session of the General Assembly, the Soviet Union supported Indonesia's challenge to their right to it. The Yugoslav delegate, explaining his vote to accept the report of the Credentials Committee, did not follow his Soviet colleague in making a reservation in favor of Indonesia's position. Neither the Soviet Union nor Yugoslavia objected to Malaysia's taking its seat on the Security Council in January 1965, in accordance with an arrangement reached one year earlier whereby Czechoslovakia and Malaysia, being deadlocked in the voting, were to share the two-year 1964-66 term. But Indonesia did object and thereupon announced its withdrawal from the United Nations, an action which Yugoslavia deplored.

To take another issue, the effort to deal with world-wide problems of trade and development through the United Nations. Partly in disenchantment with the rather meager results of their own campaign to develop trade with the third world, the Yugoslavs, after the Belgrade conference of 1961, pressed strongly for broader international action involving the advanced nations as well. The initiative in the United Nations was first taken by Yugoslavia, along with Brazil, Ethiopia, India, and Senegal, in the Economic and Social Council, which in August 1962 proposed a general conference on the subject. Pushed strongly by the underdeveloped nations, the General Assembly in the following December considered two draft resolutions. One proposed by the Soviet Union was aimed at gaining particular Soviet-bloc objectives in East-West trade, primarily the removal of Western trade controls. In support of the other draft, which was loaded with the special aims and interests of the underdeveloped countries, Yugo-

[7] U.N. General Assembly, *Official Records*, 16th Session, Plenary Meeting No. 1099, January 26, 1962, p. 1304.

slavia made a special statement on behalf of its 35 sponsors pointing out how in amended form it met some of the points raised by
the Soviet Union, the United States, and other advanced countries. In the end the Soviet delegation, in order to bolster its
influence in the third world, withdrew its own resolution and
supported the other. The United States was one of the states
voting against it because it went too far.

In the sessions of the preparatory committee for the general
U.N. conference, the Yugoslav representative played a prominent
role as spokesman for the underdeveloped nations, clashing on
several occasions with the Soviet and East European delegates as
well as those of Western nations. When the General Assembly
considered the matter again in the autumn of 1963, a group of 75
states, including Yugoslavia, submitted a draft resolution on the
forthcoming conference and with it a joint declaration stressing
the desirability of new patterns of production and international
trade as the only way in which the economic independence of the
developing countries could be strengthened. Both proposals were
adopted unanimously.

This group, which became 77 in number, held together as a
bloc through the Conference on Trade and Development
(UNCTAD), which finally met in the spring of 1964. There it
tended to dominate both the discussions and the voting. The
detailed Final Act of the conference, which contained much of
the philosophy and many of the specific desiderata of the group,
was accepted by the United States, the Soviet Union, and other
industrialized states with reservations to the effect that they must
interpret the recommendations in the light of their own statements and votes at the conference. The 77 countries issued at the
same time a declaration that the new forms of cooperation set in
motion by the conference, which were only an initial step, "must
serve as a decisive instrument for ending the division of the
world into areas of affluence and intolerable poverty."[8]

Included in the group were 76 countries of Asia, Africa and
Latin America, and one European country, Yugoslavia. On the
55-member permanent U.N. Trade and Development Board,
which grew out of the conference, Yugoslavia was chosen as one

[8] *U.N. Year Book, 1964,* p. 206.

of 22 from the group of "Africa and Asia plus Yugoslavia," not from the "centrally planned economy countries" (the Soviet bloc) or the "market economy countries." All through the long and still continuing debate on new patterns of economic relations, Yugoslavia has been squarely with the underdeveloped nations and not with the Soviet Union or with the West. If either wished to influence Yugoslavia, it could do so only by accepting the general propositions on which the Yugoslavs were at one with the third world.

Thus, if Belgrade's voice was raised against the West, it was raised in the company of many others whom the United States did not consider enemies and to whom it provided aid. Basically, our problem is not Yugoslavia's but America's relations with the third world. If the Yugoslav preference, among the third-world countries, seemed to be for those with the more radical and militant leadership and the more hostile attitudes toward the West, the ties were by no means exclusively with them. Haile Selassie, Bourguiba, and Tubman were given the same welcome in Belgrade as Abdel Nasser, Nkrumah, and Sekou Touré. At the Cairo Conference of the nonaligned in 1964 it was Tito who took the lead in arguing for coexistence and opposing Sukarno's proposals for strong and revolutionary resolutions against the West. By that time the nonaligned group had grown: 47 countries were represented at Cairo in 1964, compared to 25 at Belgrade in 1961. It was not easy to find common denominators, other than the continuing struggle against colonialism, in a group that included Indonesia, Ghana, Mali, and other militants then following Peking's line, and also countries like Lebanon, Saudi Arabia, Liberia, and Senegal. Yugoslavia found itself with India as a leader of the "moderates," stressing coexistence and negotiation with the West. The same was true among the "77" of UNCTAD, where the Yugoslavs stressed the need to enlist the willing cooperation of the developed countries.

### Yugoslavia and the Soviet Union in the Third World

So long as Yugoslav policies and activities in Asia, Africa, and Latin America are truly independent, they represent no cause for worry. If they are adjuncts of Soviet strategy, however, that is quite another matter. In support of the latter position, two theories have been advanced. The first is that the Yugoslav and Soviet parties and governments are acting in collusion to spread communism in the third world, with each playing its assigned role in accordance with an agreed strategy. The other is that Yugoslavia is acting in the Soviet interest in these areas, even though it may not know it or desire it, by the mere fact that its policies follow the line of the Soviet Union, encourage its friends, denigrate its enemies, and make Soviet policy seem respectable in the eyes of the nonaligned. There is a scarcity of conclusive evidence on the first of these theories and an ineluctable element of subjective interpretation in any answer to the second, but they are so important that they must be discussed on the basis of what is available.

We now have a ten-year record of at least superficially similar Yugoslav and Soviet policies in the third world, which during that same period has been a battleground of the cold war. It is an interesting point that each made the decision for an active policy in that area at the time when they were beginning the process of "normalization" of relations with each other. Tito made his first trip to Asia late in 1954, only a short time after the restoration of full diplomatic relations with the Soviet Union and several of its East European satellites. Khrushchev and Bulganin, while preparing the reconciliation with Yugoslavia, were simultaneously executing a turnabout in the Soviet line toward India and Egypt. Within a year of Tito's trip to Asia, they set out on their spectacular tour of Burma, India, and Afghanistan. Both Moscow and Belgrade, to judge from their public declarations, seemingly had discovered new virtues in the leaders and the policies of these Asian and African states.

After the rapprochement of 1962, the two governments spoke of their common aims. On the occasion of Khrushchev's visit to Yugoslavia in 1963, a high point in the era of good feeling, much was made in official speeches of the identity of views on all essential questions, and one of the subjects discussed was "cooperation in rendering assistance to developing countries,"[9] though with-

---

[9] From an article in *Borba*, September 5, 1963.

out any published indication of what concrete forms that cooperation would take. Tito's visit to the U.S.S.R. in 1965 produced
a joint statement expressing support of peoples struggling to win
national liberation or to protect their independence against the
imperialist states. A highly placed Yugoslav wrote of "a further
closing of the gap between certain positions of the nonaligned
policy and the policy of the socialist states." The agreement constituted "a complete confirmation of the basic theses of the policy
of nonalignment," and "must be interpreted as an expansion of
the zone of progressive policy of far reaching importance."[10] Did
Moscow, perhaps, see it as Yugoslav acceptance of the Soviet
concept of a "zone of progressive policy"?

On the surface, the two lines ran almost parallel. One must,
therefore, look as closely as possible at the motivation of Yugoslav policy and, even more, at its effects, especially as they related
to the interests of the Soviet Union and of the West. Much of the
verbiage of official Yugoslav statements need not be disinterred.
It is sufficient to stress the themes of a similar experience with the
new nations in struggles for liberation, common views on world
problems, antipathy to aggression and war, respect for independence and equality of states, and the right to economic development.[11] Since the nonaligned of Asia and Africa displayed a
bewildering variety of political and social systems, the Yugoslav
approach to them spoke more of rights and of self-determination
than of ideology and the victory of socialism. Many of the same
terms were used by the Soviet Union. To see the significant
differences, it would be useful to look at four specific cases: Egypt
and the Middle East, Algeria, the Congo, and Cuba.

EGYPT AND THE MIDDLE EAST

Yugoslavia's close relations with Egypt took form in 1955 and
1956, the same period in which Western positions were being
battered by the combined onslaught of an aroused Arab nation-

[10] Josip Djerdja, "The Only Possible Way to Act," *Review of International
Affairs,* July 5-20, 1965, pp. 4-5.

[11] As Tito did, on the eve of his first visit to Asia in a report on foreign
policy to the Federal People's Assembly, October 25, 1954. See Josip Broz-
Tito, *Borba za Mir i Medjunarodnu Saradnju, 1954* (Belgrade: Kultura,
1957), pp. 325-326.

alism, headed by Abdel Nasser, and a new and more active Soviet strategy. The great breakthrough, for Khrushchev and for Nasser, was the arms deal of September 1955 which put an end to the Western monopoly on the supply of arms to the area. The Yugoslav government upheld Nasser's sovereign right to purchase weapons wherever he liked. The real problem, in the Yugoslav view, stemmed from the efforts of Western powers to draw Middle Eastern states into "military arrangements of a bloc nature."[12] This was a position in full concord with that of Egypt. It meant acceptance of a greatly increased Soviet influence in the Middle East. But it did not mean, to Tito any more than to Nasser, favoring the extension of Soviet control or the Soviet alliance system into that region. One important factor ignored in all official comment was that this intensification of the cold war, denounced in the abstract, made it possible for Egypt, like Yugoslavia, to make positive neutralism a practical and profitable policy.

In the Suez crisis of 1956 the Yugoslav government consistently supported President Nasser. It approved his nationalization of the Suez Canal Company as a legitimate exercise of sovereignty. It opposed the efforts of the Western powers, including the United States, to work out a scheme for putting the canal under international control. When Israel, England, and France took military action against Egypt at the end of October 1956, Yugoslavia strongly supported action through the United Nations to put an end to it. Throughout the whole affair, however, Yugoslav diplomacy and published comment took care to differentiate between American policy and that of Great Britain and France, applauded American leadership in the United Nations, and gave no support to Soviet threats to take unilateral military action.

During the post-Suez period American relations with Abdel Nasser again became strained. American attempts to build strength against Soviet imperialism in the Middle East by means of the Baghdad Pact, the Eisenhower doctrine, and special relations with individual countries ran athwart the Egyptian leader's

[12] Address of Koča Popović, State Secretary for Foreign Affairs, to the Federal People's Assembly, November 12, 1955, *Review of International Affairs*, November 16, 1955, p. 5.

policy of rallying the Arab world to the banner of his brand of Arab nationalism. The events of 1958, when Syria and Egypt joined in the new United Arab Republic, civil war broke out in Lebanon, and revolution overthrew the pro-Western regime in Iraq, brought American prestige to a low point. They were grist to Nasser's mill and to Tito's also. They were hailed in Belgrade as defeats for the West's policy of cold war and blocs. After the revolution in Baghdad, Yugoslavia hastened, along with the Soviet Union and other East European states, to establish diplomatic relations and conclude trade and aid agreements with the new government of Abdul Karim Kassem. But this move was taken to support nationalism and neutralism, not the extension of Soviet influence; at that point Soviet-Yugoslav relations were at the climactic point of the second break, and Moscow had just "postponed" substantial credits previously promised to Yugoslavia.

In more recent years, since Abdel Nasser undertook his venture in Yemen in 1962, Belgrade's unofficial pronouncements have given him moral support and berated "reactionary" forces opposing the "progressive" republican regime in Yemen, whether Arab rivals like Saudi Arabia and Jordan or the Western powers supporting them. Caution, however, has kept Yugoslavia from active involvement. It is assumed that the "progressive" forces are always right but, aside from the U.A.R., it is not always easy to know which are the progressive forces. In Syria or Iraq, for example, how is Belgrade to judge the successive *coups d'état* by which army officers, Baathists, Nasserites, anti-Nasserites, and other "revolutionary, progressive elements" combine with or replace each other in power? The Yugoslavs, accordingly, have tried generally to steer clear of inter-Arab strife. They have also stayed discreetly out of Arab quarrels with states such as Turkey or Iran, where Belgrade has its own interests, not necessarily parallel to those of Cairo. This is true even with respect to Israel, which Yugoslavia recognized in 1948 and supported for admission to the United Nations. When the love affair with Egypt began in the mid-1950s, Tito refrained from rushing to Nasser's side on the Palestine question. Yugoslavia, as a close associate of the U.A.R., has not been impartial, having subscribed to many declarations about Arab rights in Palestine; but in general its conduct toward Israel has been correct, and trade between the two countries has flourished.

The United States has had difficulty enough in trying to work out a constructive relationship with the United Arab Republic and the forces of Arab nationalism not to be sensitive to one-sided criticism from Belgrade. Yet it would be foolish to draw any dire conclusions from that. Yugoslavia is not really present as a major factor in the Middle East. America's policies are determined in the light of its own interests, the ambitions, interests and actions of other powers directly concerned, and of the emerging forces in the area itself. Dealing with Abdel Nasser has been an especially difficult and still unresolved problem because of our judgment, or misjudgment, of those forces; and because of Abdel Nasser himself, not Tito.

It is well to remember, too, that Yugoslavia, as a member of the United Nations, has had a part in attempts to safeguard peace in the Middle East. When the U.N. Emergency Force was established in 1956 to oversee the withdrawal of British, French, and Israeli forces and to patrol the frontier in the Gaza area, Yugoslavia was among the first to provide soldiers to serve on it. Yugoslav military officers also took on, together with Canadians, the impossible job of observers on the border between Yemen and Saudi Arabia in 1963. In each case they were performing a service for the United Nations as a world organization, with no favor to any individual states, large or small. Unlike the Soviet Union, Yugoslavia has paid its dues and assessments for peacekeeping, and it did not support Moscow's attempt to weaken the authority of the Secretary-General.

Presidents Tito and Nasser conferred on seventeen different occasions between 1955 and mid-1966. There is no doubt that they have discussed frankly and at length their respective relations with the Soviet Union, and that Nasser has learned something from Yugoslavia's experience. Over the course of the years both have had good and bad moments with Moscow, yet none affected the cordiality of their relations with each other. Both, in fact, have played the same game of accepting Soviet aid and standing firm against interference with their internal affairs or their foreign policies. The United Arab Republic, in obtaining its supply of arms solely from the Soviet Union, is in a position of greater potential danger to its independence of policy than Yugoslavia has been since 1948. It is hard to believe that Abdel Nasser put his country in that particular position on Tito's advice.

Similarly, if one looks at the political and ideological factors, the one ascertainable fact is that all interested parties proclaim a devotion to socialism. But Nasser's "Arab socialism" bears no relation to the socialism practised in the Soviet Union. Soviet officials and writers, depending on the tactical line of the moment, alternately ridicule it as unscientific and praise it as an encouraging step on the non-capitalist road. As Nikita Khrushchev said during his visit to the U.A.R. in 1964, he would like to hear a bit less about the fraternity of Arabs and more about the fraternity of workers and peasants against the class enemy. The Soviets are prepared to work with the present regime in Cairo because it suits their strategy to do so. The Yugoslavs, on the other hand, take "Arab socialism" at face value as Egypt's way suited to Egyptian conditions.

Broad contact has taken place between Yugoslav and U.A.R. officials on various levels. The latter have studied Yugoslavia's institutions for possible adaptation to their own environment. But there are no patterns, Soviet or their own, which Yugoslav Communists are trying to get the U.A.R to follow. No agents or parties controlled from Belgrade play any part in Arab politics. The whole burden of the Yugoslav approach is that it preaches no doctrine except that of separate roads based on local history and local conditions. Its influence goes to encourage the Arab states in their independence of the Soviet Union and China, as of the West.

## ALGERIA

Algeria, like Egypt, has had a special place in the hearts of the Yugoslav leaders. Here was a people—the only people in the Middle East or Africa—who fought a long and hard guerrilla war for their independence, one which reminded the Yugoslav partisans of their own war of national liberation. During the struggle they gave what aid and comfort they could, in the form of public sympathy with Algeria's National Liberation Front (FLN), support of their cause at the United Nations, and shipments of arms and other supplies to the nationalist guerrillas. After the FLN formed a "Provisional Government of the Algerian Republic" in 1958, Yugoslavia gave it *de facto* recognition. For the Yugoslav leadership, support of the Algerian cause was primarily a question of sentiment and principle rather than of calculated nation interest. The Algerian movement was nationalist and anticolonialist. When it won independence, it showed itself to be neutralist and socialist. The attraction for the Yugoslavs to mother this newly born country was irresistible.

Even before the Evian agreements brought independence to Algeria in 1962, its "provisional government" participated on an equal basis with 24 sovereign governments in the summit conference at Belgrade in September 1961. Yugoslavia gave it formal recognition at that time. The final declaration of the conference pledged "all possible support" to Algeria's struggle for independence and expressed gratification that it was represented at Belgrade by "its rightful representative, the Prime Minister of the Provisional Government of Algeria."

The "rightful representative," Ben Youssef Ben Khedda, was soon to be pushed aside by Ahmed Ben Bella in the struggle for power that immediately followed independence in 1962. Yugoslav enthusiasm for the new Algeria did not flag, however, especially as Ben Bella showed a real interest in Yugoslavia's own experiments on its chosen road to socialism. When Ben Bella visited Belgrade in 1964, he was greeted by Tito as "a dear and desired friend," and replied that "in you, in your people, . . . our people recognize themselves." "Your friendly people," he said, are "engaged on the only correct road of building socialism . . ."[13] Large numbers of Yugoslav technicians, economic advisers, and political representatives were sent to help in the building of "Algerian socialism." Ben Bella modeled his system of self-management, applied to property taken over from departing Europeans, at least in part on the Yugoslav example. Yugoslavia, consequently, achieved a special position in Algeria, extending

[13] Tanjug dispatch, March 6, 1964.

beyond the physical proportions of the actual aid it provided; and Algeria, in turn, enjoyed Tito's consistent support in matters of foreign policy.

Ben Bella's foreign policy, like Abdel Nasser's, was strident, flamboyant, ultranationalistic. He had pretensions to leadership of the Arab West, the Maghreb, where Algeria was the largest and potentially the strongest state; and also to leadership of nationalism and anticolonialism in black Africa, for which Algeria could serve as a source of inspiration, a haven for revolutionary leaders, and a training ground for soldiers of liberation. Algerian representatives were among the most militant spirits in the Arab League and in the Organization of African Unity.

Since much of this frenetic Algerian activity in the field of foreign affairs was directed against one Western power or another, and often against American policies in particular, the United States had no reason to look kindly on it, or on those states which encouraged it. Among the latter were the Soviet Union and Communist China, in addition to Yugoslavia. Far from working together, each had an Algerian policy of its own. The Soviets and Chinese, both of whom were pouring in military and economic aid, were rivals for influence in Algeria, and each wished to use that country as a conduit for spreading influence elsewhere in Africa. Yugoslav assistance, and Yugoslav ambitions, were on a much smaller scale. Yugoslav cooperation, indeed, could be accepted by Algiers as less dangerous than Soviet or Chinese aid because it came from a small power and because the Yugoslavs dealt only with the government and the FLN, not with any local Communists.

Since the Soviet-Chinese dispute has imposed itself on nearly all aspects of relations between Communist states and those of the third world, Yugoslavia's message in the Maghreb has come closer to that of the Soviet Union than in earlier years. Both preach coexistence and the peaceful path to socialism. That is not to say that there is identity of policy and action or that Tito is an apostle of Soviet policy. The Yugoslavs had no part in the clash of Soviet and Chinese strategy centering on the Afro-Asian conference, the "second Bandung," which was to have been held at Algiers in June 1965. As advocates of the nonaligned grouping (which includes neither Russia or China) in contrast to the Afro-Asian grouping (from which Yugoslavia as a European state is excluded), they were just as glad to see the conference come a cropper after the unexpected overthrow of Ben Bella.

Ben Bella had outlawed the Algerian Communist party in December 1962 soon after coming to power. It was more a French than an Algerian party and was loyal above all to Moscow. The Soviets accepted that setback and urged all Communists to join the FLN, Algeria's single party. Yet the Algerian leaders could never be sure that Moscow would not use the local Communists against their government even while it was receiving Soviet arms and economic aid and was playing at revolution, to Moscow's benefit, elsewhere in Africa. When Ben Bella fell and the new regime of Colonel Houari Boumedienne started off by repudiating its predecessor's adventurous foreign policy and ridding itself of the curious coterie of Marxists who had been Ben Bella's closest advisers, Moscow-oriented Communist sources throughout Western Europe were loud in their protests. The Soviet government, however, kept a discreet silence and eventually accepted the new regime and renewed its aid. But all was not friendship and trust between Moscow and Algiers. A delegation from the FLN, which attended the Twenty-third Congress of the Soviet Communist Party in March 1966, walked out ostentatiously and returned to Algiers when a representative of the still-outlawed Algerian Communist party was officially seated.

Yugoslavia, also, was shocked by the overthrow of Ben Bella but for different reasons. Tito had great esteem for him as a close friend and one of the prominent figures of the third world. It was not that Yugoslav strategy had gone wrong but that a myth, which meant much to the Yugoslav leaders, had been punctured.

## THE CONGO

More serious from the American viewpoint was the Yugoslav role in the affairs of the Congo. In Belgrade, as in Cairo, the confused events of 1960 and 1961 were regarded as a simple conflict between good (in the form of the "Congolese nation" led by Patrice Lumumba and then by Antoine Gizenga) and evil (in the form of the Belgian colonialists, their imperialist patrons, and their local puppets such as President Joseph Kasavubu and Moïse Tshombé). Yugoslavia, like the U.A.R., unreservedly adopted the cause of Lumumba at a time when the Soviet Union was obviously counting on him as the instrument for establishing a foothold of its own in the former Belgian territory. It denounced "foreign intervention" by Belgium and the West, criticised the United Nations and its Secretary-General for bowing to it, and withdrew the pilots and technical personnel it had contributed to the U.N. operations in the Congo. It took the lead within and outside the United Nations in pleading and pushing its anti-Western views. After Lumumba's fall and his murder, Belgrade established diplomatic relations with Gizenga's shadow regime at Stanleyville as the only legitimate government of the Congo—one of a handful of Communist and African states to do so—while the United Nations and the great majority of its members continued to deal with the central government of Kasavubu and Cyrille Adoula in Leopoldville. Yugoslavia changed its position only when the Gizenga group faded away and the Adoula government in Leopoldville was recognized even by the states of the Soviet bloc, and then invited Premier Adoula to the Belgrade Conference of September 1961.

Again in 1964, when a series of revolts broke out in the Congo after the U.N. forces had been withdrawn, the Yugoslav government immediately injected itself into the conflict as a supporter of the "popular forces" against the central government, at that time headed by Tshombé, the particular villain in the more extreme African nationalist version of the Congo drama. Because the United States saw in the ability of the Leopoldville government to maintain its authority the only chance for relative stability, it did not look tolerantly on those states which expressed their support of the rebels by diplomacy, propaganda, or the actual shipment of arms. Communist China and the Soviet Union, acting for the most part *sub rosa,* were in that group. Algeria and the United Arab Republic, whose arms came from the Communist world, were in turn the main suppliers of arms to the rebels. Yugoslavia was an enthusiastic cheerleader. And when the Belgian-American airdrop took place in November 1964, to rescue Europeans in danger of massacre at Stanleyville, thousands of students staged a demonstration in Belgrade.

The Yugoslav government did not wish to strain its relations with the United States irreparably. Neither did it intend to apologize for the attitudes and policies which had brought relations to such a low point. The Yugoslav position, officials would explain, was based on principle. They believed national self-determination and the ending of colonialism to be principles they could not betray; therefore, they acted accordingly. If Communist China or the Soviet Union took the same stand, that was not Yugoslavia's fault. It was up to the Western powers to stop playing the neocolonialist game, to repudiate the white supremacists, the Tshombés and their mercenaries, and to live up to principles which they themselves professed and had accepted in the United Nations Charter.

There was obvious disagreement on the facts and what they meant. The United States, though it could not deny that Tshombé's use of white mercenaries was the factor that made possible his victory over the rebels, could not accept the theory that tribal dissidents stirred up against Leopoldville for one reason or another were "the Congolese people." If Yugoslav Communists chose to think of them as a national liberation movement of stalwart partisans struggling against foreign occupying powers and their local quislings, the United States could not accept that interpretation, even though it was not easy to say what the "facts" really were over a broad piece of Africa little known to Yugoslavs and Americans alike.

In a situation where the Soviets and Tito's close associates among African and Asian nationalists were all on the same side, it would have been extraordinary to find Yugoslavia on any other side. In the last analysis, the simmering down of the Congo crisis put this particular difficulty in Yugoslav-American relations into more sober and realistic perspective for all concerned. Actually, Yugoslavia's support did not appreciably help the Congo rebels' cause, nor did it contribute very much to Soviet strategy, which in this case was unsuccessful.

CUBA

In the early years of the Castro regime the Yugoslav Communists welcomed the appearance of a "socialist" regime in the Western Hemisphere and looked forward to having a new recruit in the camp of the nonaligned states. They denounced the United States for the attempt to overthrow Castro by the ill-fated Bay of Pigs adventure. Cuba participated in the Belgrade Conference of 1961, where its president, Osvaldo Dorticós, spoke in fiery phrases against American imperialism, and the final declaration of that conference objected to the U.S. base at Guantánamo as a gross violation of Cuban sovereignty. But Castro's regime did not tarry long in the status of a nonaligned country. It was moving rapidly, by the end of 1961, into a position of heavy economic dependence on the U.S.S.R. Despite jockeying for power between Castro's own "26th of June" movement and the old-time Communist leaders with long records of loyalty to Moscow, there was no swerving in Castro's growing alignment with the Soviet camp and in his desire for close ties with Communist China as well. In this situation Yugoslavia's relations with Cuba underwent a gradual but perceptible change.

Fidel Castro is comparable to Marshal Tito in that he is a self-made leader who led his own revolution and, despite Cuba's economic dependence, cannot be called a tool either of the Russians or of the Chinese. They have had to deal with him by negotiation, not by issuing instructions. On the home front he and his intimate advisers, rather than outside Communists, made the basic decisions, and the big mistakes, in determining Cuba's road to socialism. In international relations, however, the Castro line is quite different from Tito's. The essence of Cuban foreign policy is total hostility to the United States. Cuba thus became, almost inevitably, a partner of the Soviet Union in the cold war. It did not join the Warsaw Pact or any formal military alliance, but it received public pledges of Soviet military support against an attack by the United States. It gloried in being given a place in the front rank of the "struggle against the imperialists." Consequently, the Yugoslavs saw Castro as one who was sharpening the cleavage between the blocs, instead of working to reduce tensions as they were. They also wished to have good relations with Venezuela and other Latin American countries which Castro regarded as his enemies. And they did not propose seriously to damage their relations with the United States for the sake of "socialist solidarity" with Cuba. When the Soviet-bloc countries proposed a resolution in the U.N. General Assembly charging the United States with plans of aggression and acts of intervention against Cuba, Yugoslavia along with most of the Afro-Asian group abstained from voting; only Cuba and ten Communist States voted for it.[14]

Castro's international policy, moreover, was frankly revolutionary. His interest was in stirring up revolt in Latin America, in exporting his own revolution by providing training and arms to revolutionaries in other countries. Such activity was pursued in Latin America and even in Africa, from Algeria to Zanzibar, where it ran parallel to the efforts of the Chinese Communists to spread the revolution. Castro, indeed, was out in front of his Soviet allies in much of this missionary work, for the Kremlin and its established Communist parties in Latin America were much more cautious, more anxious to perserve their assets and work toward popular fronts with other parties than to risk all in armed revolts which could not succeed. As for the Yugoslav Communists, they had no use at all for such attempts to spread socialism by force. They would have liked to see the Latin American countries move toward a nonaligned position. In his trip to Latin America in 1963 Tito visited only those countries which had showed some signs of doing that: Brazil (under the Goulart regime), Chile, Bolivia, and Mexico. In all of them he talked of friendly cooperation between governments, not of socialism and revolution. He did not go to Cuba, but topped off his trip with a friendly visit to Washington. At the Cairo Conference of the nonaligned in 1964 the final declaration, bearing the stamp of Yugoslavia's moderating influence, urged only that the United States negotiate the evacuation of the Guantánamo base with the Cuban government.

The differences between Yugoslavia and Cuba, simmering for several years, came sharply to the fore on the occasion of the tricontinental conference of socialist states and "people's movements" held in Havana in January 1966, an outgrowth of earlier conferences of the Asian-African Peoples' Solidarity Organization, at which a Yugoslav front organization had been repre-

---

[14] U.N. General Assembly, *Official Records,* 16th Session, First Committee, Meeting of February 15, 1962, p. 437.

sented. The Yugoslavs strongly resented not being invited to participate or even to send an observer to Havana, thanks to the opposition of Communist China and Cuba, although the Soviet Union, presumably as an Asian power, was very much present as a leading participant.

The conference produced some militant resolutions supporting revolutionary action against the imperialists and their reactionary puppets throughout the third world, probably more militant than the Soviets would have preferred, but they did not wish to be put in the position of appearing less interested in the revolutionary cause than the Cubans and the Chinese. The Yugoslav Communists, not being able to state their case for nonalignment and coexistence at the conference, made it clear in press articles, which set off an angry exchange between *Borba,* an official Yugoslav paper, and *Granma,* the organ of Castro's party. The latter accused the Yugoslavs of being "historically frozen by passivity, inaction, opportunism, and appeasement," and of acting as "lackeys of imperialism."[15] The Chinese and the Cubans were quarreling at the time, but yielded nothing to each other in their hatred and contempt for Yugoslavia. It is ironic that the remaining trickle of Yugoslav trade and shipping to Cuba was made the occasion for a decision by the U.S. Congress to cut off all credits to Yugoslavia under the Food for Peace program.

### Conclusions

In judging Yugoslavia's role in the third world, the United States would do well to maintain a relatively calm and detached attitude. The principal cause of irritation has been the series of positions taken by the Yugoslav government running counter to American aims and policies, and its public picture of America as a power scheming to destroy the independence of new nations. The United States has seen its interests as a great power very much involved in such questions as whether countries of Asia, Africa, and Latin America can be protected against Soviet or

[15] See especially *Borba,* January 17, May 7, 9, 1966; *Granma,* February 13, May 5, 6, 1966; Radio Havana, March 9; see also *Komunist* (Belgrade), January 20, February 24, 1966; *Politika,* February 17, 1966.

Chinese intrusion, whether these countries can work out their own destiny, whether the United Nations can play a constructive role, and whether racial conflict and chaos can be avoided. It has seen Yugoslavia often following an ideological line bearing little relationship to the facts of the situation and making it more difficult for the United States, its Western associates, and the United Nations to carry out the necessary constructive policies. That may be a one-sided view, especially as it may appear to deny a small nation the same right to pursue its own interests as it sees them, anywhere in the world, that a big nation claims for itself. But it is a fact of world politics of which the Yugoslavs should take account.

Perhaps Yugoslavia's tendency to make Olympian pronouncements and send its diplomats and propagandists into action on every international issue all over the world will fade when President Tito is succeeded by men of less heroic mold. This assertiveness is a reflection of the remarkable success which the leadership and the country have had in maintaining an independent and influential position in the face of the most formidable challenges. Even if there is no major change in this respect, the record shows that Yugoslav opposition to American policies in the third world is more annoying than alarming. It has not changed the course of events. It may have been at times encouraging and helpful to our adversaries, but not in any crucial sense. On the other side of the ledger are the many occasions when Yugoslav policy has been helpful to Western interests and to the United Nations. Yugoslav votes in the United Nations, as we have seen, have by no means coincided consistently with those of the Soviet Union.

In recent years, the third world itself has undergone some striking changes both in its solidarity and in its pretensions to world influence. In 1960 the prestige of the group of Tito, Nehru, Nasser, Sukarno, and Nkrumah was at its height. Since then, India has been attacked by China and got precious little support from its partners in nonalignment, and Nehru is now gone. Sukarno and Nkrumah have been repudiated by their own peoples. Nasser has involved himself in a foolhardy adventure in Yemen. Ben Bella has been overthrown. Mrs. Bandaranaike has been voted out of power. It is hard to see the nonaligned states acting as a powerful world force in the coming years, except on the question of their economic development. That is the really crucial issue for them and one on which they need to work with the West, not to defy it.

The Yugoslav Communists have found it hard to believe that these things could have happened, so strong was their conviction that the radical nationalist leaders represented the hope of their peoples and the wave of the future. But they are nothing if not adaptable, as they have shown in their own policies at home. Yugoslavia does have a long-term interest in cooperation with the nations of Asia, Africa, and Latin America, and that interest should survive past ties with individual leaders. As practical cooperation goes on, it should rest less on ideological concepts based on socialism or anti-imperialism, less on any affinity between Yugoslav aims and the great-power interests of the Soviet Union (unless the Soviet Union itself shifts further away from a policy of using "national liberation" movements to wage cold war against the West), and more on a common effort for economic progress.

The thrust of Communist policy and influence into the third world is in three separate strands: the Chinese, the Soviet, and the Yugoslav. The range, in their effects on Western interests and on the peace and security of third-world nations, is from violent to peaceful, from revolutionary to moderate. To some extent, all strands contribute to the general trend of anticolonialism and "national liberation" which has swept these continents in the past decade. But what counts is the content of policy, not the words. To the extent that Moscow, in its duel with Peking, has become more moderate, its line has come closer to that of Belgrade. But the salient fact is that the three are rivals rather than partners, outside the Communist world as they are inside it.

## Chapter VI

# Titoism: Influence
# in Eastern Europe

International communism, ever since its birth as a political movement, has borne within it the seeds of inevitable conflict between central control and national autonomy. Any movement based on a doctrine of historical determinism was bound to have its factions and its heresies, both within its constituent parties and between them. Because the Second, or Socialist, International was never more than a loose federation of parties, it was not surprising that it broke on the rock of nationalism in the First World War. The Third, or Communist, International (Comintern) differed in that it had a power base, Soviet Russia, and a center of authority in Moscow. That fact increased its chances of success, but it did not settle for all time the question of the ultimate control of the Communist movement of the future. Failure of the revolution to spread beyond the borders of the old Russian Empire, however, and especially its decisive defeat in Germany in the early 1920s, clouded that issue because of the disparity between the one dominant Soviet party and the many other parties which had no power at all, and generally no legal existence, in their own countries.

During the interwar period Stalin made the Comintern and the world's Communist parties (except the Chinese) instruments of Soviet policy. He could crush heresies in the international movement just as he did within the Soviet Union. Many foreign Communist leaders disappeared in the purges of the 1930s; in

1938 he disposed of the entire Polish leadership and dissolved the Polish party.

In building "socialism within one country" Stalin was in fact establishing "national communism," but without ceasing to picture the Soviet Union as the indestructible base for the ultimate victory of communism everywhere. Leaders of the other Communist parties of Europe were his agents. Since they had no way of reaching power except with Soviet help, they saw no contradiction between their countries' interests and those of the Soviet Union. They were quite ready to accept Stalin's dictum that the test of any man's loyalty to the revolution and to his country's true interest was his attitude toward the policies of the Soviet Union. Thus, Tito served Stalin as an organizer of the traffic in Communist fighting men to Spain in the 1930s; Georgi Dimitrov, future ruler of Bulgaria, served him as Secretary-General of the Comintern. During the Second World War a whole group of European Communists in the Soviet Union prepared for the day when, with the entry of the Red Army into Europe, they would take power in their home countries. The dissolution of the Comintern in 1943 did not change the situation, for the management of the "liberation" was to remain in Soviet hands. One of Stalin's motives in dissolving it was to improve relations with his Western allies, but he also wanted to make sure that when the Communist parties took governmental authority in Eastern Europe he could control them directly and individually; the Comintern, though it had been a pliant Soviet tool in the past, might not be so pliant in the changed circumstances.

Victory in the Second World War, according to the Soviet version of history, enabled the forces of socialism to triumph in new areas, formerly under the capitalist and fascist yoke, beyond the borders of the great socialist fatherland. The Western powers, protesting the denial of self-determination to the peoples of Eastern Europe, saw the Communist takeover as the extension of Soviet power, through Soviet-controlled regimes, to the heart of Europe. Stalin, whatever his official propaganda said, saw it the same way; and so, we may be sure, did most of the East European Communists who were occupying the seats of authority in Warsaw, Budapest, Bucharest, and the other capitals recently liberated from the Germans. Yet this very extension of the Soviet empire to include formerly independent European nations with strong traditions of national history and culture changed the nature of the Communist world. Henceforth the Soviet leadership would be dealing with Communist regimes in power, not merely with parties seeking power. Since most of them were in power by courtesy of the Soviets and needed Soviet backing to stay there, the contradictions did not immediately appear. But there was one regime in Eastern Europe which did not fit the pattern.

The Yugoslav experience during the war, we have seen, had its own special character. Tito and his partisans fought against Hitler largely by themselves, with more help from the West than from Russia; they won their own civil war, though with an assist from the Red Army in Serbia; they developed a tremendous pride and confidence in themselves. They had unpleasant experiences and disagreements with the Russians during the war regarding aid which they did not receive and advice which they did not take. In the immediate postwar period there were differences over Yugoslavia's territorial aspirations, its plans for federation with Bulgaria and Albania, and its desire for a leading role in the Balkans. The Yugoslavs regarded these aims in absolute terms, as a matter of right, while the Soviet government had to look at them in the context of the whole range of its tactics in dealing with the West and with other Communist states. The solidarity of the Communist world was a fine thing to show as a façade to the West, but the reality of the Yugoslavs' relations with the Soviet leadership was a story of disillusionment and frustration well before the break in 1948. All this was background which made the "impossible" action of June 1948, an open split in the monolithic Communist movement, not only possible but perhaps inevitable.

Tito's defiance was recognized by all concerned for what it was: a challenge to the existence of a Communist empire run from Moscow. The heart of the challenge was in Eastern Europe, where nationalism, as in Yugoslavia, had been for more than a century the central theme of political life. Non-Communist parties had been destroyed or suppressed, the final blow coming with the coup in Prague earlier in 1948. But national resentment against Soviet domination was not far below the surface, and within the local Communist parties divisions between "Muscovites" and the more locally attuned leaders and members had already appeared.

Wolfgang Leonhard, then an East German Communist functionary trained in the Soviet Union, gives a vivid account of the impact of the dispute between Yugoslavia and the Cominform on those who had begun to question Stalin's all-embracing wisdom. As Marxists, they had scorned and ignored all Western arguments and revelations as propaganda, but the reply of the Yugoslav Communist party to the Cominform resolution "had the effect of a bombshell." "Any one in the West," he has written, "must find it difficult to realize what an impression was made on us by the passages . . . which condemned the habit of servile subordination and refused to admit errors which had never been committed. These were things on which the whole system of criticism and self-criticism rested—indeed the Stalinist system as a whole. For me it was like a revolutionary banner . . ."[1] Titoism, in its simplest form as the right to national independence and equality within the Communist world, was a virus which, because it kept a Marxist character and cited Lenin in defying Stalin, penetrated into the bloodstream of the Soviet system in Eastern Europe. It attacked vulnerabilities in the very puppet regimes which the Kremlin had put in power, in ways that no Western propaganda or diplomacy could do.

Stalin's way of fighting off the virus, by having his henchmen carry out drastic purges of leaders who might be potential nationalists or Titoists, checked but did not destroy it. His insistence that the accused "traitors," most of them more popular than the subservient Communists who judged and condemned them, had schemed and plotted with Tito served only to advertise Tito's defiance. And his failure to overthrow Tito in Yugoslavia meant that the whole problem would have to be faced by his successors, without his authority and without his means of action.

[1] Wolfgang Leonhard, *Child of the Revolution* (Chicago: Henry Regnery Co., 1958), pp. 390-391.

The manner in which they dealt with Tito and with Titoism in Eastern Europe had the effect of encouraging throughout the region the same forces of national communism that existed in Yugoslavia. Laszlo Rajk in Hungary and Traicho Kostov in Bulgaria, "Titoists" executed in the Stalinist purges of 1949, were given "posthumous rehabilitation." Whether Stalin's successors could have avoided that trend is doubtful. They could hardly have suppressed it by force. Accordingly, they chose to compromise, and by compromising with Titoism in 1955 they opened wide the door to its influence in Eastern Europe. The shattering effect of Khrushchev's anti-Stalin speech in February 1956 spurred it further.

One can identify various specific ways in which Yugoslav influence was exerted: through radio broadcasts, through party and professional connections which were opened up after Tito's visits to Moscow and to some capitals of Eastern Europe, through study of Yugoslavia's institutions by Polish and other economists, and by the demonstration of the benefits in Western aid and international fame brought by independence. As Poland and Hungary were most affected by Eastern Europe's "thaw" in 1955 and 1956, it was on their writers and their more nationalist party members that Yugoslav influence made its deepest mark. When Wladyslaw Gomulka re-emerged from obscurity in 1956 to take a leading role in the Communist party, Poles remembered that he had been purged in 1949-51 specifically on grounds of sympathy with Tito and the Yugoslav heresy. When Imre Nagy wrote down his own philosophy after being ousted from power and from the party by the Stalinist Rákosi in 1955, he stressed his conviction that Hungarian communism must be independent and national in content, like Yugoslavia's, or there was no chance of its acceptance by the people.[2]

### Lessons of 1956

The events of 1956 in Poland and Hungary grew out of the experience of those two nations, and of the Soviet reaction to

[2] Imre Nagy, *On Communism* (New York: Frederick A. Praeger, 1957), pp. 20-42, 244.

them. Yugoslavia had no determining role. Yet the connection with Yugoslavia was obvious, for resistance to Soviet domination, whatever the difference in the course of events and the immediate outcome in the two countries, sprang from the same cause as Yugoslavia's earlier resistance. Gomulka's strong stand for independence, in a dramatic confrontation with the new Soviet leaders at Warsaw, was comparable to Tito's defiance of Stalin eight years before. In the case of Hungary, where the rule of Rákosi had been especially offensive to Tito, the Yugoslav leadership was frankly desirous of a change and so informed Khrushchev. Rákosi's dismissal was in part a sacrifice to Tito. His successor, Ernö Gerö, of the same Stalinist stripe and not Tito's choice, returned from a visit to Belgrade to run straight into a revolution.

The Yugoslav government openly approved the initial revolt in October 1956 which brought Imre Nagy back into office. What happened thereafter turned this happy ending to ashes, for it was not the end. The further course of the revolution swept the Titoist solution aside and left but two alternatives: a nationalist Hungary in which communism or a Communist party would have little place, if any, or a Communist Hungary in which Soviet control would be restored and a new subservient regime put in power. As Tito said in a remarkable admission, the blindness of the Stalinists had unfortunately created a situation in which reactionaries came to the fore; the "justified revolt" against the Stalinist clique "turned into an uprising of the whole nation against socialism and against the Soviet Union." Soviet intervention and Western inaction then decided matters in favor of the second alternative, which he accepted as regrettably "necessary" in the circumstances; otherwise, there would have been "a terrible civil war, in which socialism could be completely buried and in which a third world war could break out."[3] The last thing Tito and his colleagues wanted was more violence spreading across frontiers. Not only the Nagy regime in Hungary

[3] See his major speech at Pula, November 11, 1956, *Borba,* November 16, 1956. English translation in Paul E. Zinner (ed.), *National Communism and Popular Revolt in Eastern Europe* (New York: Columbia University Press, 1956), pp. 516-541.

but their own brand of socialism in Yugoslavia might not survive that.

In spite of what happened in Hungary, Tito remained confident that time was on his side. The process which began in 1948 in Yugoslavia and was continuing in Poland, he felt sure, could not be held back by the Stalinists, neither by those still active in the Soviet leadership nor by those in the Communist parties of Eastern Europe. He had faith in Nikita Khrushchev, whom he pictured as a friend of necessary change still hampered by Stalinist elements but with the tide running in his favor. "I believe that the events in Hungary will probably be the last tragedy necessary to jolt the Soviet comrades and leaders who are still blind to this in other countries into doing everything in their power to prevent such a situation as now prevails in Hungary from arising in other countries as well." Yugoslavia's task was neither to retreat into its shell nor to try to undermine other East European governments, but to collaborate with the Polish Communists and other forward-looking elements and even with the new Kádár regime in Hungary (this, when Imre Nagy was still a refugee in the Yugoslav embassy in Budapest), to work in the ideological field through contacts and talks, "and thus to insure the victory of the new spirit."[4]

### The "Socialist Commonwealth"

One can pick any point in time between 1956 and the present, measure the temperature of Soviet-Yugoslav relations and compare it with the varying degrees of independence shown by the individual states of Eastern Europe. In general, when Moscow and Belgrade came closer together, the "new spirit" of which Tito spoke made headway in at least some of the states of the Soviet bloc. When Yugoslav "revisionism" held a high place in Moscow's catalogue of enemies of the socialist camp and threats to its solidarity, especially in the years from 1957 to 1961, the tendency was for the others to close ranks at Moscow's command. The new era of good feeling in Soviet-Yugoslav relations since 1962, coinciding with the dispute between the Soviet Union and

4 Same, pp. 531, 534-536.

Communist China and with the growing independence of such outside Communist parties as the Italian, has seen a further loosening of the bonds between Moscow and its satellites, to the point where in some cases even the term "satellite" can be questioned as accurately reflecting the complex set of relationships which has developed.

The Yugoslavs watched with interest Khrushchev's efforts to find a substitute for the Stalinist system in Eastern Europe after 1956. The "socialist commonwealth,"[5] which was to take account of differing national conditions in the member states while preserving the essential points of socialist cooperation and Moscow's primacy of leadership, was a brave and probably genuine attempt to find a middle way between the Titoist concept of voluntary cooperation among equals and the requirement of a central source of authority and decision. Khrushchev was apparently willing, also, to allow all the satellites the very large measure of autonomy that Poland already had. The Yugoslavs could applaud Khrushchev's flexibility in trying such an experiment. But they could not regard it as meeting their own concepts so long as regimes that were essentially Stalinist remained in power in Czechoslovakia, Bulgaria, and Albania, nor when the new commonwealth expressed its solidarity, at the behest of the Soviet leadership, in attacking Yugoslavia's policies and its party program. The experiment might possibly have succeeded, if Khrushchev and his colleagues had been granted a period free of crisis. It had no chance once the whole "socialist camp" was struck by the open Chinese challenge to Soviet primacy.

The conflict with China also gave Yugoslavia a new chance to make its influence felt. Following various gestures of Soviet-Yugoslav friendship in 1962, the Yugoslav party renewed its direct contacts with the Soviet and East European parties. Yugoslav representatives attended the congresses of the East German party in 1963, of the Polish party in 1964, the Rumanian in 1965, and the Soviet and several others in 1966. At the East German congress a fierce attack on Yugoslavia by the Chinese representative

[5] The term *sotsialisticheskoe sodruzhestvo* was first used and broadly defined in the Soviet government's statement of October 30, 1956, issued at the height of the Hungarian crisis. For text, see Zinner, cited, pp. 487-489.

brought down upon him a barrage of whistles and catcalls from all the pro-Moscow delegates. The Yugoslavs' participation, as far as the evidence shows, meant no change of line on their part. They have given no ground on the essential point of independence. The fact that they can join in the "international workers' movement" to this extent is an indication that the movement is not what it used to be. "Proletarian internationalism," the touchstone of which is solidarity with the first country of socialism, is still a slogan under which other East European states may rally loyally to a current Moscow line.[6] Yugoslavs are more likely to invoke it for such proposals as the encouragement of tourism among socialist states.

When an occasion arises where the Soviets try to make a meeting serve as a demonstration of conformity with their own policies, the Yugoslavs either are not invited or purposely stay away. So it was with the conference of March 1965, called to line up as many Communist parties as possible behind Moscow's course in dealing with China. So it is with all meetings connected with the Warsaw Pact, which Yugoslavia never joined, and all collective declarations of policy against the West. Yugoslavia may wish to denounce the West and often does, but does so either alone or in the carefully drafted bilateral communiqués which issue from Tito's incessant exchanges of visits with leaders of countries both inside and outside the Soviet bloc.

### Diversity in Eastern Europe

It has now become banal to say that the Communist world is no longer a monolith; that its central ideology has eroded; that no one Communist state has the same status or situation as the others; that the Soviet Union no longer exercises control over the East European governments in any complete sense or tries to do so; that all are moving in one way or another toward greater

---

[6] See, for example, the article of Zoltán Komocsin, Secretary of the Central Committee of the Hungarian party, on "National Interest and Internationalism," *Népszabadság*, March 24, 1966 (translation by Radio Free Europe), and Kádár's speech at the Twenty-third Congress of Soviet Communist party, March 31, 1966.

autonomy; that polycentrism and revisionism and diversity have carried the day. This is indeed the trend of the times. Such is the situation in the Communist world today that it has not been necessary to defy Moscow in order to gain a wide freedom to deal with domestic matters. But the trend should not be overestimated to the point of saying that all the East European regimes defied the Soviet Union to assert full national independence. They remained in the Soviet security system, and some still saw in the Soviet Union the ultimate guarantee of their survival.

The Polish Communist leaders still have the fundamental elements of control over internal affairs which they won in 1956, but their international policies, after showing some signs of independence for a brief period after the October days, relapsed into conformity with the Soviet line. (There are, of course, reasons of geography and national interest underlying those policies, not just subservience, but the solidarity with Moscow goes well beyond national interest.) Hungary, despite the repression of the revolution, managed to reach a situation where the despised Kádár, imposed on the country in 1956, won Soviet tolerance to pursue a conciliatory course with his own subjects and thus to reduce his earlier total dependence on Moscow. Czechoslovakia, under Antonín Novotný, a Stalinist-type leader clever enough to survive the wave of de-Stalinization, has been pushed by its own severe problems to deal with them in its own way and not according to any Soviet model or advice. Bulgaria's leadership, except for one rather ludicrous abortive attempt in 1958 to make a "great leap forward" on the Chinese model, long seemed the most reluctant to take any initiative or to change its satellite status, partly because of its own weakness; but even the Bulgarian Communists, especially since a nationalist-inspired attempt at a military coup threw a scare into the regime in 1965, have shown signs of a more independent line and of seeking national coloration. The Rumanian regime, long considered docile, surprised the world with its decisions to oppose economic integration of the Soviet bloc, to play a role of its own in the dispute with China, and to cut down Soviet political and cultural influence within Rumania. Finally, Albania's Stalinist leaders, fearing for their own future in Khrushchev's new commonwealth, took their country out of the Soviet bloc altogether and rallied to Peking.

The picture has been confused by the fact that two trends, one toward greater autonomy for the satellite states and the other toward greater internal liberalization and attention to the desires of the population, have been taking place under the general label of de-Stalinization, but they do not always run parallel. Diverse situations developed in different countries. Hungary had more internal liberalization than Rumania, but Rumania went farther in asserting an independent foreign policy. Poland in 1956 took a big jump forward but has since largely lost its position as front-runner by retreating on both fronts. It is often forgotten that removal of the symbols and some of the substance of Stalinism was pressed on certain East European states—Czechoslovakia, Rumania, and Bulgaria in particular—by Khrushchev himself. While liquidating many aspects of the Stalinist system in the Soviet Union, he could not afford to see the "cult" survive elsewhere in the commonwealth. Thus, some of the early steps of liberalization in those countries were not acts of revolt against Soviet influence but rather a reluctant yielding to it. Since Khrushchev's fall, the attenuation of Soviet influence has continued more or less without reference to the issue of Stalinism.

Because Yugoslavia led the way by declaring its independence in 1948 and then liberalizing its internal system in open rejection of Soviet theory and practice, but still within the bounds of continuing rule by the Yugoslav Communist party, it is easy to see why the eyes of those who led the movement for change elsewhere in Eastern Europe were on Yugoslavia. Few were ready, in the early years, to admit that they saw there any model for their own countries. It was not healthy to follow openly in the path of those being denounced, or who might later be denounced, as revisionists and traitors. Later, when Moscow accorded Yugoslavia the respectability of the term "socialist state," all kinds of relations, party and governmental, were renewed between Belgrade and the East European capitals.

Increased trade and industrial cooperation made East European economists and managers aware of the workings of Yugoslavia's "market socialism" and its workers' councils. The economic reforms discussed at length in Czechoslovakia, Poland, Hungary, and Bulgaria in the early and mid-1960s grew mainly out of the failures of the centralized systems in those countries, but the ways in which Yugoslavia had already shifted to a decentralized system entered into many of the discussions. There was no intention of copying the Yugoslav model, especially since the Yugoslav economy itself was staggering at that time. While Tito's achievements and Yugoslav courage were admired, in the countries of Central European tradition like Poland, Czechoslovakia, and Hungary there was some reluctance to accept the idea that a more backward and less "civilized" Balkan nation had anything to offer them in the way of experience and leadership. More important than direct borrowing of institutions was the infection of Eastern Europe with the spirit prevailing in Yugoslavia, where the freedom of inquiry and of experimentation was greater than in any other country ruled by a Communist regime.

It has been argued that Titoism is a spent force as an influence in the Communist world; that the other East European states and the Soviet Union itself, having abandoned Stalinism, will work out their own process of change without paying much heed to a country which no longer represents a challenge and has not even made a notable success of its over-advertised separate road to socialism. Such arguments gloss over the continuing influence of Yugoslavia's real independence and of its role as vanguard—to use a Communist term—in the adaptation of communism to the practical realities of the modern world both in domestic and in foreign policy. It still poses a challenge, in 1967 as in 1958 or 1948. Exploration of a new position for the Communist party in the state and the society and drastic economic reforms are opening the way to theories and practices which can only be called arch-revisionism. These changes are no reversion to conformity. They carry a message to other East European nations.

### Rumania and Yugoslavia

Rumania's relationship to Yugoslavia is a special case. The two countries are traditional friends. Once their common frontier was settled by compromise after the First World War, they became allies in the Little Entente and Balkan Entente. When Yugoslavia was attacked and carved up in 1941, Rumania, then a German ally, took no part in the attack and no share in the partition, as Hungary, Bulgaria, and Albania did. Relations were strained during the period of Stalin's cold war against Tito but lacked the bitterness of those between Yugoslavia and its other Cominform neighbors. Although Rumania remained fixed in the Stalinist mold all through the 1950s, Yugoslav observers, for reasons not apparent to the less initiated, expected an eventual assertion of independence by that country.

Whether the Yugoslavs gave the Rumanian leaders any direct encouragement in their bold resistance to Khrushchev's plan of economic integration of Eastern Europe and the Soviet Union through the Council of Mutual Economic Assistance in a "great socialist market," we do not know. But it is interesting that in the same period when the Rumanians were deciding their course the two states were in touch with each other on the huge Iron Gates navigation and power project which had long been a dream on both sides of the Danube. They worked it out on a bilateral basis, without any reference to the CMEA and without counting on Soviet help. The Soviet Union did agree later (March 1965) to provide equipment to both countries for electric power plants and other installations, but that would fill only a fraction of the needs, and the possibility of some financing by the World Bank or Western countries remained open. Rumania's top leader, President Gheorghe Gheorghiu-Dej, paid a formal visit to Belgrade in November 1963, and both presidents met again at the Iron Gates in September 1964 to inaugurate construction.

There was no doubt that the Yugoslavs were pleased at the turn of affairs in Rumania, and that they saw the parallel between the Rumanian Communist party's "statement" of April 1964 and their own answer to Stalin and the Cominform in 1948. The statement contained a great deal of harsh talk against the West, which was customary, and an explanation of Rumania's position in the Soviet-Chinese dispute, but at its heart was a clear expression of policy that was pure Titoism:

There does not and cannot exist a "parent-party" and a "son-party," parties that are "superior" and parties that are "subordinate," but there exists the great family of communist and workers' parties, which have equal rights. No party has or can have a privileged place, or can impose its line and opinions on other parties.[7]

In foreign policy, Gheorghiu-Dej succeeded in winning a considerable freedom of action by avoiding total identification with Moscow in its quarrel with Peking, by expanding Rumania's economic and cultural relations with China and with Albania while the other East European states were contracting theirs, and by assaying a mediator's role in the Soviet-Chinese dispute. These specific policies bore no relation to Yugoslavia's, but the staking out of an independent line followed the Yugoslav model. In 1963 and 1964, moreover, Rumania began to cultivate ties with Western Europe (especially France), to seek advantageous economic deals in the United States, and to take independent positions at international conferences, no longer slavishly following the Soviet lead.

Gheorghiu-Dej's successors extended his policy of independence to the point of declaring their distaste for blocs, *all* blocs. There was no sudden withdrawal from the Warsaw Pact, such as Hungary had attempted in 1956. There was no public espousal of the Yugoslav type of nonalignment. But it is significant that Nicolae Ceauşescu and the other Rumanian leaders had Marshal Tito as their guest for a lengthy visit just a few weeks before Ceauşescu's memorable speech of May 9, 1966, stressing Europe's need for a loosening of blocs on both sides, praising France for its assertion of national sovereignty, and denouncing past instances of Soviet dictation to the Rumanian Communists.

One is always in danger, when trying to analyze communications among Communists, of taking the ideological argument too seriously and overlooking the factors of power and national interest behind it. Tito's fight with Stalin, which he did not seek, was more than a dispute about Marxist doctrine, which was the

[7] *Statement on the Stand of the Rumanian Workers' Party concerning the Problems of the World Communist and Working Class Movement, endorsed by the Enlarged Plenum of the C.C. of the R.W.P.* See Supplement to *Documents, Articles and Information on Rumania* (Bucharest: Agerpress, 1964), pp. 49-50.

language of their written exchanges. It was more, even, than a conflict over which Communists, Stalin's or Tito's, were going to control the territory and population of Yugoslavia. The fight was about national independence, and Tito in waging it did so in defense of the right of the people of Yugoslavia not to be ruled by an outside power. A cynic might say that it mattered little to the people whether their oppressors were foreign or native Communists. In fact there was a difference, because the Tito regime in making the struggle had to depend on the people and had to meet some of their concerns if it was to be won. Under the impact of the struggle for independence, the new Yugoslav political and economic system took form as a series of changes—gradual, limited, and often reluctant—by which the regime took greater account of the wishes of the people.

The same considerations apply elsewhere in Eastern Europe, where nationalism runs deep. The successes of October 1956 were won by Gomulka, by those Communists who supported him, *and* by the Polish people. He could not have done it without the people behind him, and it was touch-and-go whether they might not push things too far for the possibility of compromise, as the Hungarian people did. They saw Gomulka as a man who could stand up to the Soviets and could give more freedom at home. He did just that, and though some of the concessions to the people have since been withdrawn, much of the substance of the gains of 1956 still stands.

In Hungary, the revolution of that year was a national uprising. Although it was put down by force, the situation did not revert to the Stalinist system of Rákosi. On the contrary, the regime of János Kádár granted some of the things for which the revolution had been fought: not political freedom or national independence, the major goals, but an easing of the party dictatorship, the satisfaction of certain material wants, and a greater freedom of expression. The decision to make such concessions was more than *noblesse oblige*. It was the combined result of popular pressure and the regime's need to get enough cooperation to make the political and economic system work. Help from the Soviet Union, which Kádár got, was not the answer to his major problem.

In Czechoslovakia, also, popular pressures had a great deal to do with the regime's retreat from Stalinism and its espousal of major economic reforms. In its own quiet way Czechoslovakia may be going further than any of the others toward new institutions more suited to the needs and the wants of its people. Thus national communism, in Czechoslovakia and Hungary as in Poland and Yugoslavia, was not just a device by which local Communist leaders could get some elbow room in their relations with Moscow. It grew also out of the problems they had in governing their own populations in an age where the simple and brutal methods of the Stalinist system were no longer adequate.

Rumania's path to greater independence was peculiarly its own, and true to its own traditions. Despite purges, there was no significant change in the leadership from the time the Communist regime was installed by the Soviets in 1945. Gheorghiu-Dej was a Stalinist under Stalin. He was a Khrushchevist in the early years of Khrushchev. But he drew certain conclusions from the loosening of the bloc, managed to get Soviet occupation troops withdrawn from the country in 1958, and maneuvered cleverly to increase Rumania's freedom of action bit by bit. He never made a move of such clear defiance of Soviet interests as to provoke a thunderous Soviet reaction or an open break.

In the quarrel with other partners in the CMEA and with Khrushchev, the Rumanian leaders defended what was basically a Stalinist policy: rapid industrialization, especially heavy industry, regardless of economic cost. It was a *national* policy, pursued without regard to Moscow's desires and intended to bring the less developed economy of Rumania to a position of equality with the more advanced countries. And it was accompanied by measures, especially in the cultural field, to assert Rumanian nationalism against Russia—measures which could not fail to be popular with the people.

The Rumanian national revival is evident in the rewriting of history, in greater freedom of literary and artistic expression, and in the rehabilitation of many figures of Rumania's past who were not Marxist or revolutionary or pro-Russian by any stretch of the imagination. Among the national traditions being rediscovered are those of the "Latinity" of the Rumanian people and their close ties with Western Europe. The Rumanian claim to Bessarabia and northern Bukovina, provinces taken by Russia in 1940, has been indirectly voiced, though not by the government. All these trends are limited and controlled by the regime. Thus far, there has been no political or economic liberalization comparable to what happened in Poland, Hungary, or even Czechoslovakia. This is why Rumania, especially if it stays in close contact with Yugoslavia, is an interesting case to watch. That Yugoslavia after the declaration of independence in 1948 still pursued basically Stalinist policies at home for a couple of years in an effort to prove its orthodoxy, and only then began to strike out on its own with reforms and innovations, is often overlooked. Rumania's independence is still limited by proximity to the Soviet Union and by inclusion in the Soviet security system, and it has not been under siege as Yugoslavia was after 1948; but the government has taken unto itself the powers of decision on how to chart a national course, at home as in foreign relations.

### Unbottled Nationalism

Nationalism, long bottled up by the authority of the Kremlin as it strove under the slogans of socialist internationalism to keep order in Eastern Europe and hold the satellite regimes under tight control, has become a force very much to be reckoned with, not only by the Soviet Union. As we have seen, nationalism has provided an area of common interest between regimes and peoples in the assertion of national aims against Soviet domination. On the other hand, it also colors the policies of governments with the national emotions and aspirations of a past era in which much of the energy of the East European nations was devoted to bitter disputes among themselves. A decade or so of "fraternal socialist solidarity" did not remove for all time the differences between Hungary and Rumania over Transylvania, intermittent polemics between Sofia and Belgrade over Macedonia, the ill feeling between Czechs and Poles, between Rumanians and Bulgarians, or the antagonism between nationalities within states like Czechoslovakia and Yugoslavia.

The governments in Eastern Europe, especially when they feel less inhibited by Soviet control, are tempted to exploit national feeling against their neighbors to increase their own popular support. They are fearful, at the same time, of unleashing forces they cannot control. Hungary, for example, has perhaps more national claims and grievances than any other nation of the region. Yet the Hungarian government handles these questions in the most gingerly way. Despite considerable provocation, it is very careful not to stir up the Hungarian people over the treatment of the Magyar minority in Rumania. The Hungarian press is full of warnings against "bourgeois nationalism" as contrary to the peoples' true interests. Undoubtedly the Hungarian leaders have in mind the outburst of nationalism in 1956, when the Hungarian people hunted down Communists, cut the red stars out of the national flag, and sought to liberate Hungary not only from Soviet control but from the Communist system as well.

Whatever the regimes do, nationalism is a factor of prime importance for the future of Eastern Europe and for Yugoslavia's relation to it, especially in the Balkan area. If one looks back to the period between 1941 and 1948, when fraternal Communist parties were supposedly cooperating in the war against Hitler and in the struggle against "bourgeois" elements, it is now clear that the Yugoslav and Bulgarian parties could not settle their differences over Macedonia and over the terms of the new federal relationship by which they proposed to bring their two countries together. These disputes were brought before Stalin for solution, but were not solved by the time he lost whatever authority he had over Yugoslavia.

Tito, during this same period, was apparently struck with the vision of a Balkan federation or wider union in which Yugoslavia would have the dominant or leading role; it would include Bulgaria, Albania, Macedonia (possibly including parts of Greece if the guerrilla war in that country should be successful), and perhaps Rumania and Hungary.[8] Tito made no such proposal openly, but it is interesting that Dimitrov of Bulgaria did, after concluding an agreement with Tito in 1947 which apparently

---

[8] See Stephen D. Kertesz, "American and Soviet Negotiating Behavior," in S. D. Kertesz and M. A. Fitzsimons, *Diplomacy in a Changing World* (Notre Dame: University of Notre Dame Press, 1959), pp. 150-151.

provided for the eventual inclusion of a separate Macedonia (made up of both Yugoslav and Bulgarian portions) in a federation with Yugoslavia and Bulgaria. When Dimitrov spoke publicly of a Balkan or East European customs union in January 1948, he was chastised by Stalin and forced to recant. Tito said nothing, but the Balkan federation idea was among the factors which convinced Stalin that Tito had grown too big for his breeches.

After the break of 1948, Stalin brought out into the open all the disputes over territory and minorities he could use against Yugoslavia. He encouraged and backed Bulgaria, Albania, Rumania, and Hungary in pressing old-time claims, in harboring pro-Soviet Yugoslav emigrés, in vicious propaganda, in the creation of frontier incidents, and in attempts to stir up revolt inside Yugoslavia. He engineered splits in the Greek guerrilla movement in order to nullify Yugoslav influence there; then the Yugoslavs wrote finis to the Greek rebellion by closing the frontier to the supplies which were its lifeline.

The frenetic revival of national antagonism did not give Stalin what he wanted. The Tito regime survived it. But this was not something that could be turned off and forgotten after Stalin's death. The disputes have been there ever since, agitated more or less at various times according to the circumstances but never really out of sight. If the various Communist Balkan states are drawn more toward nationalist policies, will they return to past patterns of conflict with each other? Or will their dynamic nationalism be turned against non-Communist neighbors? Bulgaria and Albania have historic territorial claims against Greece as well as against Yugoslavia.

Yugoslavia, by a combination of statesmanship and the pressure of international circumstances, has achieved what looks like a stable settlement with its non-Communist neighbors. The historic and apparently irreconcilable quarrel with Italy in the Adriatic, centering on Trieste, was finally settled by negotiation in 1954, with the good offices of the United States and Great Britain. Relations with Italy since then have been a minor miracle, better than anyone on either side expected. Yugoslavia's claim to territory in Austrian Carinthia was not pushed, and though the Yugoslavs maintain a concern for the Slovene-speaking people on the Austrian side of the border, relations have been stable and good. Since the end of the Greek Communist rebellion in 1949 the governments in Belgrade and Athens have succeeded in restoring the friendship that marked relations between the two countries before communism appeared on the scene. Although the Balkan alliance of Yugoslavia, Greece, and Turkey, signed in 1954, has faded into obscurity, the firm relationship between the first two has remained, despite occasional press polemics over the status of the Slav minority in Greek Macedonia. Yugoslavia has thus secured its rear, so to speak, for working out its relations with Communist neighbors.

A decade ago it appeared that the Balkan area was sharply divided into three segments (three Soviet-bloc states, the independent Communist state of Yugoslavia, and two non-Communist states allied to the West), and that each would make its way more or less independently, bent on demonstrating the superiority of its own system. That is no longer the clear pattern, what with growing diversity in the former Soviet empire, Albania's defection, the halting progress of the Yugoslav experiment and increasing Yugoslav links with Eastern Europe, and the easing of cold-war tensions across the European frontiers of Greece and Turkey. These trends should not be overestimated. Soviet influence remains strong in Bulgaria. Yugoslavia remains wedded to its own "humanistic socialism" against what it sees as rigid bureaucratism to the east and the capitalism to the south. One cannot say the cold war has subsided when Albania is still the bitter enemy of all its neighbors and when Greek Communists are obviously trying very hard to get to power in Athens. Nevertheless, there is something new in the air.

Back in 1957 the Rumanian Prime Minister, Chivu Stoica, proposed a Balkan conference, to be attended by Rumania, Bulgaria, Albania, Yugoslavia, Greece, and Turkey, with the purpose of considering the whole range of regional problems and laying the foundations for security in the area. Taken at a time when Rumania had shown no signs of independence, it was without doubt a Soviet initiative, perhaps even a Yugoslav initiative as well. At any rate, Yugoslavia publicly welcomed it, but did not follow up the idea after Greece and Turkey declined. Two years later, in June 1959, Rumania renewed the proposal for a conference and suggested that the entire Balkan area be made an atom-free zone, following a theme on which Khrushchev had held forth during a recent visit to Albania.[9] Again, Yugoslavia replied positively and Greece negatively.

Belgrade's attraction to the idea of a non-nuclear Balkan zone fitted in with the general penchant of the nonaligned nations for measures to ease the cold war and promote peace; but there may have been another reason: a desire to draw both Soviet satellites and non-Communist states with Yugoslavia into regional arrangements of a special international character. The Yugoslavs were aware of the motivation on the Soviet side, which was to draw Yugoslavia toward the Soviet bloc, as well as to break down the attachment of Greece and Turkey to NATO and to eliminate American nuclear power from the area.

As time has passed since the original Rumanian proposal, the idea of the association of Balkan nations seems to have acquired a life of its own, apart from Soviet strategy. It is not a new idea; movements for greater cooperation and even union among the Balkan states were a feature of the 1930s, and the federation schemes of the early postwar period have not been forgotten. Of recent years, a whole series of Balkan activities has taken place across the cold-war frontiers, from scholarly conferences and music festivals to athletic meets. On the political side, much of it does not go beyond statements of the virtues of peace and neighborly relations. But here we should look at the promise of such trends, not merely at their present reality, because that is where future Balkan leaders, not necessarily those in power today, may also be looking.

It is noteworthy that Bulgaria has assumed a more active role, increasing its ties with Yugoslavia and settling a series of disputes

[9] The Soviet proposals made in the joint Soviet-Albanian communiqué of May 30, 1959, and in a formal note to the governments of the six Balkan countries, Italy, the United States, Great Britain, and France on June 25, 1959, proposed an atom-free zone "in the Balkans and the Adriatic area," including Italy. See Gillian King (ed.), *Documents on International Affairs, 1959* (Oxford University Press, for the Royal Institute of International Affairs, 1963), pp. 141-144, 593.

which had clouded its relations with Greece since the Second World War, and has done these things on its own rather than under Soviet orders (though not against Soviet opposition). Without ceasing to proclaim its eternal loyalty to Moscow, even the Bulgarian Communists have given signs of wishing to have their state play a more individual international role *as Bulgaria,* not just as an echo of the Soviet Union. Yugoslavia, too, has been emphasizing its role in the Balkan region. Tito visited Sofia in 1965 for the first time since 1947, and relations have become partly unfrozen. There is no doubt that the Yugoslavs would like to see Bulgaria assert itself against Soviet guidance, as Rumania has. Even without notable progress on that score, over the long run an increasingly close Rumanian-Yugoslav combination could virtually control the Balkan area down to the borders of Greece and Turkey unless the Soviet Union should make the unlikely choice to use force to prevent it.

The case of Yugoslavia's relations with Albania is a special one, a classic example of the use of ideology to mask a national conflict. That conflict, which goes back to the time of Albania's birth as a state in 1912, rests squarely on Albania's claim to a large area of Yugoslavia populated by close to one million Albanians and on its fear of Yugoslav domination, and on Yugoslavia's concern over Albania's role as puppet of a big power hostile to Yugoslavia (Italy before and during the Second World War, Germany in 1943-45, the Soviet Union from 1948 until about 1960, and China thereafter). All the ideological arguments that have filled the air for years mean nothing unless they are translated into these simple terms.

When Albania's leaders, who never broke with Stalinism, broke with "N. Khrushchev and his clique" to ally their country with China, then the Soviet Union, Yugoslavia, and the other East European states, in deciding what to do about this perennial nuisance, had to look at the problem as part of the larger one of what to do about China. The Soviet-Chinese dispute affected all the governments in Eastern Europe, and each had to define its attitude toward it.

*Chapter VII*

# Belgrade—Moscow—Peking

Never should it be forgotten that Marshal Tito and those who rule Yugoslavia with him regard themselves as Communists. Despite the disputes they have had with other Communist states and parties, despite their manifold and often cordial relations with non-Communist nations, they have always sought to find their place in the "international workers' movement" in which their faith and their outlook was formed. To them, Yugoslavia's independence means independence as a socialist state under the guidance of the party, the League of Communists. When another socialist state, no matter how powerful, denied to Yugoslavia the right to build socialism according to its own conditions and traditions, or followed policies which threatened world peace, that state had to be opposed. Yet, in denouncing the policies of others and fighting the good fight for their own, the Yugoslav leaders had no idea of reading themselves out of the "international workers' movement." They were outside of any socialist "camp" and made clear that they despised that word, so frequently used by Moscow and by Peking, for its connotation of hegemony and blocs. But they were always working to find a place in the world's general advance to socialism, which, like the Soviet or Chinese leaders, they regarded as the wave of the future.

The program of the League of Communists of Yugoslavia, therefore, whether or not it corresponds to the reality of what is happening in the world, is important for an understanding of

Yugoslav conduct in world affairs. The program adopted at the party's Seventh Congress in 1958, confirmed by the subsequent congress in 1964, sets forth the basic thesis that socialism in its various forms is gaining ground the world over. In the West it is evident in strong workers' movements and in the trends of public policy. In the third world it is apparent in the reaching out by new leaders for socialist ways of organizing their national life. No one Communist party or socialist state, however, could define socialism for everyone or force its own brand on others. Thus, according to the Yugoslav interpretation, there was no inevitable conflict between two camps, capitalist and socialist, to be decided by one imposing its will on the other; there was no need, even, for a cold war.

Peaceful coexistence, a term used so much in the past decade that it has lost any clarity it ever had, is for the Yugoslavs more nearly a doctrine where for the Soviet Union it has been a tactic and a slogan. Nikita Khrushchev had no hesitancy in asserting that peaceful coexistence was no more than a means of carrying on the struggle against the capitalist-imperialist camp so long as certain conditions, mainly the danger of nuclear war, obtained.[1] The Yugoslav leaders, like their counterparts in Moscow, talk about the "struggle for peace" and often oppose Western policies in Southeast Asia, Africa, and elsewhere. They do so, however, not as followers of the Soviet Union or China in a strategy of conquest and subversion, but as supporters of the independence of nations having every right to find their own way, presumably to socialism. To the West, under the stress of a situation in which Yugoslavia is condemning and opposing Western policies, this may seem a distinction without a difference. But there is a difference, and the distinction is an important one going to the heart of relations with the Communist world.

Yugoslavia's experience with China since the Communists took power there in 1949 is revealing of the Tito regime's general approach to world affairs, and also of the position of a small nation trying to maintain both its independence and its socialist

[1] On Soviet use of the term, see George F. Kennan, "Peaceful Coexistence: A Western View," *Foreign Affairs*, January, 1960, pp. 171-190; Philip E. Mosely, "The Meanings of Coexistence," same, October, 1962, pp. 36-46.

label. It is a story of a dream shattered by a rude awakening, of high hopes followed by bitter disillusionment. China was distant. The Yugoslavs knew little about it. When the facts of power did not conform to their theories, they themselves recognized that it would have to be the other way round.[2]

Through all their phases the salient point about Yugoslav-Chinese relations has been that they are a function of the relationship of each to a third power, the Soviet Union. Even before the Chinese Communists gained full control of mainland China, Tito had already broken with Stalin. Naturally, they appeared in Yugoslav eyes as a great hope, for China could provide powerful backing for the Yugoslav idea of the Communist world as a grouping of independent states. The Chinese Communist party had not been under the Kremlin's control during its struggle against Chiang Kai-shek. As the government of mainland China it obviously would have to cope with conditions quite different from those of the Soviet Union. It would want Soviet help, reasoned the Yugoslavs, but it would not accept Soviet direction or dictation. It might, therefore, be a natural ally of Yugoslavia.

According to this line of thought, the Communist world could develop not as a unified bloc with a center of orthodox doctrine and authority in Moscow but, pending full development of "polycentrism," as a community with three centers. It would rest on a tripod, Moscow-Peking-Belgrade, each providing inspiration, from its own conditions and experience, for the general progress of socialism. It was a bold conception, and quite typical of the Yugoslavs that they should equate their small country with the two giants. It also had an essential validity, which later events confirmed, in the point that China was too big and too different to become a Soviet satellite and had a power base in its own army. But the hope that in these early years the new China would take the Yugoslav side in the dispute with Stalin was seriously misplaced.

Mao Tse-tung, in this ticklish period of establishing his party's rule, was not about to alienate Stalin by expressing solidarity

[2] See John C. Campbell, "Yugoslavia: The Wreck of a Dream," in A.M. Halpern (ed.), *Attitudes toward China: Views from Six Continents* (New York: McGraw-Hill, for the Council on Foreign Relations, 1966), pp. 368-388.

with Tito. A resolution of the Central Committee of the Chinese party endorsed the Cominform resolution of 1948, pointing out that "the Tito clique" had betrayed Marxism-Leninism and "fallen into the mire of bourgeois nationalism."[3] Mao then set about negotiating an alliance with Moscow. He did not bother to give the courtesy of an answer to Yugoslavia's proposal to establish diplomatic relations. The Chinese Communists, who saw the West as their great enemy, had made their decision to lean to the Soviet side, and they were well aware that the West was supporting Yugoslavia against the Soviet Union.

The Yugoslavs have never ceased to exalt the victory of the Communist revolution in China as a great landmark in world history, and to praise the Mao regime for its liberation of the people from feudalism and capitalism. They have consistently supported Peking's right to the Chinese seat in the United Nations and to a status of full equality in the councils of the world. In the early period they made the argument that China's isolation only benefited Stalin and his policy of hegemony over the socialist world. Paradoxically, it was only after Stalin died and the Soviet Union itself took the line of reconciliation with the Yugoslavs that the Chinese were prepared to take up relations with them.

Peking, by the mid-1950s, was in the Bandung phase of its foreign policy, preaching peaceful coexistence with the neutralists of Asia and Africa. It was also beginning to be interested in playing a wider role within the Communist world, including Eastern Europe. However skeptical the Chinese might be of the value of relations with Yugoslavia, it was a move that comported with the broadening of horizons.[4] The basic Yugoslav purpose was the same as before: to find support for the development of the Communist world of their imagination, a cooperative com-

[3] Liu Shao-chi, *Internationalism and Nationalism* (Peking: Foreign Language Press, 1951), p. 1. The article was written in November 1948.

[4] Later, in the course of their dispute with Khrushchev, the Chinese stated that it was he who in 1954 proposed to them that they improve relations with Yugoslovia, "for the purpose of winning it back to the path of socialism"; but that "we did not entertain very much hope for the Tito clique even then." See "Is Yugoslavia a Socialist Country?" *Jenmin Jihpao* (People's Daily), September 26, 1963.

munity of independent states. Active Yugoslav-Chinese collaboration would be a demonstration to the Kremlin that anything like Stalin's empire could never be reconstituted. The Yugoslavs, accordingly, made much of the new, more friendly relationship. They exchanged many delegations with China. They were pleased at the Chinese interest in Eastern Europe, especially the apparent encouragement given to Polish leaders in 1956 to assert their national interests against the Soviet Union. They were gratified when China welcomed the results of the Twentieth Congress of the Soviet party, at which Khrushchev had denounced Stalin, and when Chinese publications conceded that Stalin's handling of Yugoslavia had been a major error. For Tito and his followers, this was a happy and hopeful period. But it proved to be no more than an interval.

### China Turns Left

The Hungarian events of 1956 shook Peking as they shook Moscow. Both had seen the specter of disaster to the whole structure of the Communist camp. If this was where Titoism led, the Chinese were against it. They would continue to warn against "great-power chauvinism," by which they meant Soviet domination of others, but now saw the vital need of all Communist states to demonstrate their solidarity behind Soviet leadership. Chou En-lai conspicuously avoided Belgrade in his peacemaking tour of Eastern Europe in 1957. The Chinese virtually cut off the Yugoslav Ambassador in Peking from contact with government and party officials. Then at the Moscow meeting of Communist parties in November, Mao Tse-tung, although he was conciliatory toward the Yugoslav delegates and tried to persuade them to accept the general conclusions of the conference, went along with a strong antirevisionist declaration they could not accept.[5] In April 1958 the Yugoslavs went ahead with their Seventh Congress and its program, the effect of which was to confirm Moscow

---

[5] Phyllis Auty, *Yugoslavia's International Relations, 1945-1965* (mimeographed paper prepared for the Stanford University conference on Yugoslavia, 1965), p. 42. Compare Donald S. Zagoria, *The Sino-Soviet Conflict, 1956-1961* (Princeton: Princeton University Press, 1962), pp. 148-151.

and especially Peking in their conviction of Tito's incorrigible revisionism, already condemned in the Moscow Declaration. In May 1958 the Chinese let go with a violent broadside against Yugoslavia, of which the most telling blow was the assertion that the Cominform resolution of 1948 had been "basically correct."

Why this turn in Chinese policy? The Yugoslav leaders have ascribed it largely to China's own internal problems. As they saw it, the Mao regime, following the "hundred flowers" experiment with its looser rein, decided to reassert its own narrow dogma, tighten up party cadres, re-establish discipline and turn left, cutting out all liberal or outside influences and preparing to embark on a "great leap forward" in economic growth and institutional change. Strains had certainly appeared both at home and in relations with the Soviet Union, not to speak of the continuing tension with the United States. In any event, as the Chinese high command surveyed the future, it took a good look at Yugoslavia and saw no place for it as a partner inside or outside the socialist camp.

Both in domestic and in foreign policy Yugoslavia fitted the pattern of "revisionism" which had become China's bugbear. In the Chinese view, Tito had abandoned Leninism, threatened the solidarity of the socialist camp, and sold his country to the Western imperialists. What particularly infuriated the Chinese was the presumption of Tito's efforts to establish his influence with the neutralist nations of Asia. These were areas where China itself intended to be the dominant socialist power. Thus, the Peking leaders felt that they had to attack Yugoslavia. The terms on which they did so, calling Tito a restorer of capitalism and a lackey of the West, had a familiar ring to the Yugoslavs. This was the Stalinist campaign all over again, though the wave length was different and the words were not matched by action.

Tito took the bold decision to counterattack. He had to, in order to assert Yugoslavia's credentials as a socialist state. And there is no doubt that he had his eye on Moscow even more than on Peking. Although the Soviet leaders were going along with the campaign against Yugoslav revisionism and publicly disapproved of the new Yugoslav party program of 1958, they did not return to the pressures and boycotts of Stalin's time or call again for the overthrow of the Tito regime. Even their language did not match the vituperation then used by Stalin and now being used by the Chinese.

What Tito decided was to bring the whole issue before the world again for public debate. He still had faith that Khrushchev, whatever he was saying in public about revisionism, was pulling the Soviet Union in the direction in which Yugoslavia was pointing. The Yugoslav leaders decided to stress the theme of peaceful coexistence as the guide for a truly Leninist policy, a theme they thought responsive to long-term Soviet interests, no matter how cynically Khrushchev might interpret or use it as a slogan or tactic of the moment. How much the Yugoslavs knew of the developing difficulties in Soviet-Chinese relations it is difficult to say. Probably they knew a good deal. Their decision, in any case, was firm: to place before all Communist governments and parties the choice between a policy of coexistence, among socialist states and between them and other states, and the Chinese policy which offered to other peoples only Chinese hegemony and the prospect of nuclear war.

Edvard Kardelj, whose standing as a party spokesman was second only to that of Tito himself, was the man chosen to state the Yugoslav case. Entitled *Socialism and War* and published in 1960, his tract depicted Chinese policy as provocative, adventurous, dangerous, hegemonistic, sectarian, pseudo-revolutionary, and totally wrong. It had nothing to do with Marxism or Leninism, but had taken over the discredited legacy of Stalin and—crowning insult of all Communist polemics—of Trotsky. The burden of the argument was that the Chinese were trying to foist their own wrong-headed policies on other nations, and were insisting on armed revolution and war to expand the area of socialism.

In offering the Communist world the Yugoslav alternative, Kardelj did not hesitate to describe it as "the only way which corresponds to the spirit and the direct interests of socialism and present-day human civilization." This doctrine of the progressive internal development of each country within a system of peaceful coexistence, one might say, "is even the official policy of the socialist camp."[6] Use of the term "socialist camp," generally avoided in Belgrade's pronouncements, was a curious note. The

---

[6] *Socialism and War* (Belgrade: Jugoslavija, 1960), pp. 112, 147-149.

fact that no criticism was made of current Soviet attitudes, at a time when Moscow was still charging Yugoslavia with revisionism, was another. Kardelj seemed to be staking out a common front with the Soviet Union and others on the Soviet side against China. It may well be that the purpose of *Socialism and War* was not so much to tell off the Chinese as to open the way for a rapprochement with the Soviet Union.[7]

There is little question that the Yugoslav Communists were genuinely shaken by China's conduct. Brought up in the hard school of the Communist movement, toughened as they were by the experience of a war which brought a four-year nightmare of death and destruction to their country, they found it hard to comprehend the callous disregard of human life and values displayed by the Peking regime both in regimenting its own people and in risking the devastation of the world in a nuclear war.[8] Chinese power did not directly threaten Yugoslavia, although it could do so after Chinese influence became dominant in Albania. The great danger was that China and the Chinese line might win out in the Communist world as a whole.

Regardless of the merits of Kardelj's various arguments, he was right on the point that the Soviet Union's interests were not those of China. In the same year in which *Socialism and War* was published, Khrushchev clashed openly with Chinese representatives at a conference in Bucharest and withdrew all Soviet technicians from China. The Soviet government had already cut off its assistance to China in nuclear matters. The agreed Statement which emerged from the 81-party conference at Moscow in December 1960, and which incidentally condemned Yugoslav revisionism once again, only papered over the differences.

At this stage Albania defied Khrushchev and sought help from

[7] See Viktor Meier, "Yugoslav Communism," in William E. Griffith, ed., *Communism in Europe: Continuity, Change, and the Sino-Soviet Dispute*, Vol. I, (Cambridge, Mass: M.I.T. Press, 1964), p. 47.

[8] See Sonja Dapčević-Orešćanin, *Istorijske Osobenosti Kineske Revolucije* (Belgrade: Institut za Medjunarodnu Politiku i Privredu, 1964), pointing out the historical and national conditions differentiating China's socialist revolution and international conduct from those of European socialist states; same, "O jedinstvu i sporovima u medjunarodnom komunističkom pokretu," *Medjunarodni Problemi*, no. 1, 1964, pp. 9-17.

China. For a time the Russians and the Chinese avoided direct polemics with each other by aiming their thunderbolts at Albania and Yugoslavia, respectively. But all the world knew where the major targets were. In October 1961, at the Twenty-second Congress of the Soviet party, Khrushchev publicly denounced Albania, a direct challenge to the Chinese. In 1962 Moscow and Peking began their lengthy exchange of public recriminations, charges, and countercharges. Once that point was reached, Yugoslavia was no longer at the center of the stage. One of the major Chinese charges, however, was that the Soviet Union was courting that archtraitor and renegade, Tito.

The many honors heaped upon Tito when he visited Moscow in December of that year left no doubt that Khrushchev embraced him as an ally against the "dogmatism" of Mao, although he took care to mention that some ideological differences remained between Moscow and Belgrade. Tito has made clear his view that any backsliding by the Russians into agreement with the Chinese would be a "rotten compromise," betraying the fundamental principles of socialism.[9]

Yugoslav-Chinese hostility has not ceased. The Chinese Communists have chosen to ignore Yugoslavia as hardly worthy of further comment, though occasionally publishing an article to prove that the "Tito clique" has abandoned socialism and restored capitalism—in their eyes a not unnatural charge in view of the changes in Yugoslavia.[10] The Yugoslavs have lost all illusions about China as a counterweight to the Soviet Union in support of the Yugoslav view of a socialist community of mutually respectful independent states. There is no Peking-Moscow-Belgrade tripod for the Communist world. The sad experience with China has merely confirmed what they discovered in the conflict with Russia, that relations among Communist states do not work that way.

---

[9] *Peti Plenum Centralnog Komiteta Saveza Komunista Jugoslavije* (Belgrade: Komunist, 1963), p. 23.

[10] See R.V. Burks, "Yugoslavia: Has Tito Gone Bourgeois," *East Europe,* August 1965, pp. 2-14.

## *Vietnam*

One may ask why this view of Communist China has not brought Yugoslavia into sympathy with the American view on the dangers of Chinese expansion and the need to contain it, especially after China's aggressions against India, Yugoslavia's friend. As a matter of fact, Yugoslav descriptions of China's role in Vietnam bear some resemblance to those emanating from Washington. China is not concerned with the interests of the Vietnamese people but is "carrying out her well-known policy of blackmailing and endangering world peace." Its government "is against any solution in Vietnam that would bring peace and unity to this country on the basis of an independent policy and normal relations with the U.S.A." China is using and abusing the Vietnamese liberation struggle for its own global strategy, which is to expand the conflict, create conditions for "the so-called world revolution" and make impossible peaceful coexistence between the Soviet Union and the United States.[11] The difference between Belgrade and Washington is in the former's view of American policy as, like the Chinese, directed against the rights and true interests of the people of Vietnam. On this point both official statements and press articles have at times been couched in such strong language as to put added strains on Yugoslav-American relations.

In considering Yugoslav views on American policy in Asia, we run into two attitudes which are embedded in the Yugoslav leaders' view of the world. The first is the insistence on nonalignment, which dictates staying out of great-power conflicts, except to urge peace and to deplore any resort to force except clearly in self-defense. American military action against a small country thousands of miles from the United States appeared in Yugoslav eyes as a pure example of imperialism, not the less to be condemned because China also was following a reckless course. Yugoslav officials have made some pointed statements against American military action in Vietnam, especially when the United States resumed the bombing of North Vietnam in January 1966,

[11] Vojo Daković, "Chinese Policy and the War in Vietnam," *Review of International Affairs,* January 20, 1966, pp. 9-10.

but this attitude has hardly been confined to Yugoslavia, or to nonaligned states.

The second fixed attitude of Yugoslavia on the Vietnam question stems from its view of the Ho Chi Minh regime in Hanoi. Belgrade sees the "Democratic Republic of Vietnam" as an independent socialist state, not a creature of Peking or Moscow, trying to avoid domination by either while seeking, legitimately, to unify the whole nation and fighting for its life against foreign aggression: in short, the nearest thing to an Asian Yugoslavia. Enthusiasm on the Yugoslav side, however, has seldom been matched by cordiality on the other side. The history of the relationship is of some interest as it bears on the broader question of relations among socialist states.

Early in 1950, Ho Chi Minh's Viet Minh movement sent messages to a number of states, including Yugoslavia, proposing the establishment of diplomatic relations. On February 21, the Yugoslav government sent a telegram of acceptance, receipt of which was acknowledged on February 27. Within two weeks, however, the Viet Minh radio was strongly attacking Yugoslavia, following a visit by Ho to Peking, and no further communications took place. The Yugoslav leaders apparently continued to believe that Ho personally agreed with their ideas on the situation of the Communist world. More in sorrow than in anger Kardelj reported at the end of 1950 that the movement fighting for the independence of the Vietnamese people had joined the fight against the independence of another country, Yugoslavia.

Although diplomatic relations between Yugoslavia and Communist China were established in January 1955, it was not until the end of 1957, after a visit by Ho Chi Minh to Belgrade in August, replete with fulsome mutual praise by the two "comrade presidents" and tributes to their countries' progress on their respective roads to socialism, that the Yugoslavs had any success with Hanoi. Even then, it was a situation of diplomatic relations without resident diplomats, for Hanoi followed Peking in its open anti-Tito turn early in 1958. The Yugoslav chief of mission in Peking was accredited to Hanoi but never went there. The North Vietnamese ambassador in Warsaw was accredited also to Belgrade. There were, indeed, hardly any relations at all, not even public name-calling like that in which Yugoslavs and Chinese were indulging. Yet Ho's party and government were clearly on the Chinese side of that controversy.

The Yugoslav leaders, nonetheless, have continued to regard the Hanoi government and the Viet Cong as embodying the principle of self-determination. They have been sufficiently alarmed about the danger to world peace, however, to want a negotiated settlement, not a fight to the finish to impose Ho's terms. Yugoslavia has been critical of American policy and actions in Vietnam, as the Soviet Union and the Communist states of Eastern Europe have been. But where the latter have taken no public position in favor of a negotiated peace, although they would probably like to see it come about, Yugoslavia has openly and actively promoted a compromise settlement, even to the point of being denounced by Hanoi for its pains. The Yugoslavs took the lead in organizing the appeal of seventeen nonaligned states in March 1965 to the "parties concerned" in the Vietnam war to seek a political solution through negotiations "as soon as possible without any preconditions." The initiative showed considerable moderation, both in the terms proposed and in the manner of handling them. The North Vietnam regime dismissed it as "inappropriate" because it did not conform to Hanoi's own "four points" for settlement of the conflict (which included American withdrawal and settlement of the affairs of South Vietnam "in accordance with the program of the National Liberation Front").[12] While hailing the stated conviction of the Soviet government and Communist party that the war's outcome must be complete victory for the National Liberation Front of South Vietnam on the basis of "four points," North Vietnam has flayed Tito for his "vile maneuvers" on behalf of American imperialism.

It is natural for Washington, with its fierce concentration on Vietnam, to judge the policies of other states by the extent to which they seem to be with us or against us in that struggle. The United States would do well, however, to take a long-range view

[12] Text of appeal of seventeen heads of state or government, April 1, 1965, in *Yugoslav News Bulletin* (New York), no. 340; North Vietnam's reply broadcast by Hanoi radio, April 19, 1965.

of Yugoslavia's position and possible influence. However the present phase of the struggle in Vietnam comes out, the United States is not likely to stay there forever with large military forces and a decisive voice in political affairs. Eventually, there has to be some determination of the country's future by the political forces existing there, whether by free elections or in some other way. In the long run, the West will want to see a Vietnam which is independent and not a satellite of China. This is also the aim of Yugoslavia.

No one can say for certain whether a Communist regime in Vietnam would be Titoist. Obviously, in the midst of the present struggle the United States cannot simply abandon the field on the assumption that a victorious Hanoi regime would assert its independence against China. The removal of American power from the Southeast Asian scene would make that outcome all the more unlikely; Yugoslavia's successful stand for independence after 1948 was not unrelated to the balance of world power. Yet the attempts of Hanoi to balance Chinese and Soviet influence and the divisions within its own leadership are indications of a desire on the part of some to keep as much independence as possible in a situation where help from China is indispensable. There is no reason to assume that the Vietnamese people, Communist or non-Communist, would willingly accept Chinese domination. If there were a settlement of the present struggle providing for self-determination and sufficient protection in the form of international guarantees, they might not have to.

Should matters develop in that direction, the political influence and example of Yugoslavia might have a significant role to play, and it would not be for the purpose of helping to extend Chinese domination, but to block it. Yugoslavia's present policies could well contribute to its capacity for such a role. While that possibility may not be of much comfort to Americans today as they read official Yugoslav statements about the "imperialist aggressors" in Vietnam, present damage to Western interests— in fact, little more than an annoyance—should not blot out all thought of compensating benefits in the future.

## Chapter VIII

# Titoism: The Home Front

In a book devoted to international relations, Yugoslavia's domestic scene cannot and need not be described in detail. But there is an inescapable connection. The very word "Titoism" has been used for both internal and external policies. Inevitably, too, it evokes the question of political succession: What happens to Titoism after Tito? Do current trends point to a crisis, or to some fundamental change?

Shortly after the break with Stalin the Yugoslav Communists set out to build their own political and economic system, one which they felt was suitable to their country's conditions. They built it piece by piece, often adapting the ideology to fit the concrete measures they found necessary or desirable to take. For over fifteen years they have continued to build, and to experiment, frequently in times of stress approaching crisis when the ideal has had to yield to the practical, and the long-range to the immediate. Nevertheless, some definite trends are discernible which may throw light on Yugoslavia's future, both internally and in the international context. Does Yugoslavia's system offer anything in the way of a transition to new forms of socialism in which the people will have a greater share in government, greater civil liberties, and freedom of expression? Will it add to the attraction of independence for other East European states? Can it, through its emphasis on the human and democratic aspects of political and social relations, help lead the way toward a softening of the ideological conflict between East and West and toward basic settlements in Europe?

The first changes after 1948 sprang mainly from the desperate situation in which the Tito regime found itself. Under severe pressure from outside, it had to keep the country going. It had to keep up production of food, weapons, and other goods. These aims were hardly possible of attainment so long as the Yugoslav people were subjected to the pressures of the old system such as collectivization, which was intensified after the break. The regime learned in time that it had to conciliate the people if it wanted their loyalty and support. To use the police and security apparatus to round up "Cominformists" was necessary; but it was just as necessary to ease public pressures on the population. Many rigid methods and ambitious schemes of the old era were abandoned. The five-year plan was given up. The economic organization of factories was changed. Peasants were allowed to leave collective farms, and they did, *en masse*. The old constitution of 1946 was drastically modified in 1953. Coincident with these changes, the Yugoslav Communists joined battle with Stalin on behalf of their own road to socialism. From that time forward they never again looked to the Soviet Union as a model. They rather expected the Russians to learn something from them.

### The Workers' Councils and the New Economy

The first fundamental economic reform, the law of 1950 establishing workers' councils in industry, apparently stemmed more from ideological than from strictly economic motives. Party spokesmen were accusing Stalin of having turned the dictatorship of the proletariat into a dictatorship over the proletariat by creating a system in which industries were owned by the state and managed by the bureaucracy. Their own system, by contrast, was to rest on the concept of "social ownership" by the whole people and management of each factory by a representative council of its own workers. Turning over complex decisions to people without much formal education or experience in industrial management hardly seemed the best way to improve production, but the change was not as sharp as it appeared on paper. The workers' main concern was the size of the pay check rather than policy and management. Each factory had a director, usually a Communist, and each workers' council had a group of leading spirits, usually Communists, with the result that basic policy remained largely in the hands of the party, which could exert its influence also through the trade unions and various "front" organizations.

If outside observers did not always take the Yugoslav experiment in industrial democracy seriously, the Yugoslav leaders themselves did. They committed themselves more and more to the system of workers' councils as a showpiece of their own form of Marxism. That the councils rarely functioned in strict accordance with the laws and regulations, and not at all in accordance with official propaganda, was less significant than the fact that they did function. With the parallel reforms toward decentralization of economic policy, putting important powers in the hands of individual enterprises, the councils began to deal with such critical matters as the distribution of profits and the amount and direction of investments. Individual industries and plants began to develop interests of their own not wholly tied to the party line or controlled by the party. Even if in only a limited way, the councils represented progress toward the participation of workers in the economic system. No such progress was apparent in any other socialist state or "people's democracy" supposedly being led by the vanguard of the proletariat.

Whether by force of the Yugoslav example or of the propaganda flowing from it, the idea of workers' councils won some support in Eastern Europe. In Poland, after the events of October 1956, the Gomulka regime experimented with them, but by 1958 they were stifled by amalgamation with trade unions and party organizations. In Hungary, workers' councils sprang up from below during the revolution. They showed surprising strength in the workers' resistance which continued after the Soviet intervention and the fall of the Nagy government. These were revolutionary "soviets" which had no opportunity to develop as part of the economic system, for Kádár got rid of them as soon as he could.

The Yugoslav influence, both in Poland and Hungary, was

unmistakable. And the workers' councils continue to be a subject of discussion in Eastern Europe, especially where decentralization and economic reform have come to be the order of the day. Khrushchev himself, while visiting Yugoslavia in 1963, expressed interest in the councils and said that they were deserving of study. But this particular public utterance did not make its way into print in the Soviet Union.

It is not necessary or possible at this stage to pass any definitive judgment on the workers' councils. The system is now anchored in the constitution of 1963. Since the big problem for Yugoslav industry is efficiency, the councils may be a brake rather than a stimulus to rapid progress. Yet they are important as a symbol that the system can develop new kinds of institutions not wholly in the pattern of strict and total control by a ruling party. Call it evidence of a kind of pluralism, or of the "direct democracy" the Yugoslav leaders profess to be building. It is at least a proof that there is something different, and potentially much different, about their brand of socialism.

The development of workers' councils has been tied to a general policy of economic decentralization, which also began in the 1950s. They served as protective coloring for giving managers a freer hand as against the central bureaucracy. The leaders found that the system of detailed planning and total control of the whole national economy from the center was not producing results. They decided, therefore, to give individual enterprises a greater freedom to invest capital, to plan their production, to market their products, and even to make their own arrangements with foreign firms for international trade. The reform had a markedly encouraging effect on production and on those engaged in it, especially the plant directors. It also brought into being a new type of commercial firm devoted to buying, selling, negotiating, and performing other functions suitable to a free-market economy.

The central government kept control, at first, of a large proportion of the investment capital. It continued, by setting price and wage levels and rates of exchange, to determine the general directions of the economy in accordance with its over-all plan. Yet the sum total of "liberalization" was considerable. It had its negative side in that the interest of an individual plant or locality was often put ahead of broader national interests. There was not the kind of really free initiative and competition in the domestic market that could have developed a stronger and more resilient economy, although the rate of industrial growth continued high. But again, as in the case of the workers' councils, it was a basic modification of the old system. Even a limited devolution of authority to the level of the individual enterprise was a healthy contrast to the tight dictatorship maintained before.

Unlike the workers' councils, which became a fixed part of the ideology, the idea of decentralization was never left without challenge. From the standpoint of the League of Communists, it was a good thing when it showed results in increased production and prosperity. But it was not an unmixed good if the diffusion of powers of decision in economic matters tended to undermine the party's control of the country. This point was always in the background when economic policy was under consideration, even in the technical arguments of economists on the relative merits of central planning and dependence on free market forces. At times when the national economy seemed to falter, as in 1962 or again in 1964, voices in the party invariably were raised against liberalization and decentralization as responsible for it, with the conclusion that a return to party discipline and central control was the only answer. Indeed, there was a basic split in the ranks of the party on this question, with Tito as a sort of balance wheel keeping policy from veering drastically to one side or the other.

It is hard to avoid the conclusion that the issue of economic organization is crucial to Yugoslavia's "separate road" and to the whole future of the country. The speeches and resolutions of the Eighth Congress of the League of Communists, held in December 1964, frankly recognized the difficulties and reflected some sharp differences of opinion among the leaders. The main question was whether those difficulties, many of which could be attributed to the way the decentralized system had been working, could be overcome by a retreat or by a further advance. A political battle had to be won before the question could have an answer. The decision, apparent from the nature of the reforms which followed the congress, was against any return to unadorned centralism. The "liberals" were to be given a chance. Some said it would be their last chance.

### The Reforms of 1965

The immediate reasons for the reforms of 1965, as a veteran Yugoslav economist has pointed out, were economic: inflation, idle capacity in industry, failure of the government to find workable policies on prices and investment, weakness in foreign trade.[1] The intent was to meet those difficulties by drastic measures to increase productivity, to provide a freer domestic market, and also to bring Yugoslavia into the world economy on a competitive basis. Individual enterprises were to keep their wide freedom of decision. They were to have more investment capital at their disposal through the banking system rather than from the federal government. But they were also to make their own way without a protected home market and government subsidy. If they could not, they might have to shut down and throw many people out of work, with consequent dangers of political unrest. The devaluation of the dinar (from 750 to 1250 to the dollar) was to help make these things possible. Internationally, the dinar was to become real money.

If the reforms were bold and risky, it was all the more significant that they were tried. The decision showed the effect of fifteen years' experimentation with the forms and methods of an open economy. Although the outcome was recurrent crisis rather than unmixed prosperity, it only increased the feeling in important sectors of society and regions of the country that liberalization had to be continued and expanded, that an attempt to reverse gears would bring a major economic and political disaster. Hence, the extraordinary spectacle of Tito and other party leaders calling for free play for economic forces unhampered by the constraints of political decisions.

If Yugoslavia were a richer and more homogeneous country,

[1] Rudolf Bićanić, "Economics of Socialism in a Developed Country," *Foreign Affairs*, July 1966, pp. 633-650.

the economy might have surged ahead under the impetus of the initiative of enterprises and the spur of competition in a relatively free market. But it is a country of limited resources. The Tito regime came to power in a backward peasant economy which had suffered great losses and damage during the war, and the new leaders compounded their difficulties by their own inexperience and doctrinaire approach. Nevertheless, Yugoslavia has made remarkable economic progress in the past twenty years. The rate of industrial growth has been generally high, at times spectacular. The standard of living is about twice that of the 1930s.[2] Yet with all the expansion, all the reforms, all the foreign aid which has poured in, formidable difficulties remain: low productivity in industry, disappointing agricultural output, and a continuing deficit in the balance of international trade (although tourism and remittances from Yugoslav workers abroad have recently brightened the balance-of-payments picture). The leaders have discovered that a high rate of investment and of industrial growth does not necessarily mean healthy economic progress; and that where growth is built on governmental subsidy of uneconomic plants, eventually there comes a reckoning.

As in other Communist societies, agriculture has lagged far behind industry, partly because governments put their capital resources into industry by preference, partly because incentives for peasants to produce were never sufficient. In spite of the Yugoslav regime's surrender to the peasants in the early 1950s, allowing them to leave the collective farms, and its later decision to invest more in agriculture, the problem remains unsolved. Every year in which the weather is not wholly favorable—and that has meant virtually every year—the country is unable to feed itself and must import large quantities of grain. The regime holds to the principle that collectivization will not be imposed, but it still bestows its favor and its investment funds on the

[2] This estimate is for the population as a whole. Some groups, particularly the former upper and middle classes, saw their standards fall drastically through the directed social revolution. Many elements (real wages, consumption, housing, social security, etc.) go into any measurement of living standards. See the discussion in George W. Hoffman and Fred Warner Neal, *Yugoslavia and the New Communism* (New York: Twentieth Century Fund, 1962), pp. 361-381.

"socialist sector," largely state farms (less than 10 per cent of the arable land, but much of it in the most fertile regions) and restricts the size of private farms. Not until the mid-1960s was the individual farmer freed of burdens and restraints which prevented his getting a fair market price for his products.

Of all the problems, that of the more backward regions, which is closely tied to the controversial debate on liberalism and centralism, has presented the most formidable difficulties. Many new industries were established by central or local decision in Bosnia, Montenegro, and Macedonia for primarily political reasons. They increased employment there, but those which were unprofitable and had to be subsidized constituted a continuing drain on the rest of the country. Naturally, this burden has been resented by the peoples of the better endowed and more productive republics. Inevitably, the nationality question has intruded itself into economic policy.

Whereas before the Second World War that question, especially the Serb-Croat dispute, was at the center of politics and threatened the very existence of the state, the Communists have controlled its disruptive force, thanks to a combination of concession (the system of federal republics), repression, and the bitter memory of the horrors of mutual slaughter during the war. Yet the conflicts remain, not only among the unreconstructed Serb or Croat nationalists and among the people, but within the ranks of the party itself. Much of the controversy is on the middle and lower levels, but also among the leaders; within the solidarity and discipline of the party, it is recognized, for example, that Vladimir Bakarić speaks for Croatia, Petar Stambolić for Serbia, and Lazar Kolishevski for Macedonia. Even Marshal Tito's two top lieutenants for many years have always had national labels, for no Yugoslav ever forgets that Aleksandar Ranković, formerly the heir apparent, is a Serb (and became publicly a "greater Serbian chauvinist" after his fall from grace), or that Edvard Kardelj is a Slovene. Only Tito himself stands above it all.

Decisions on economic policy affect the attitudes of these men and of the people in Yugoslavia's separate regions. For example, centralism is favored by those who speak for the less-developed areas in the south and east, because it is the only means by which they, through political influence, can gain the subsidies and development funds they want. Those are the areas where most of the "political" factories were located, and from which many of the party stalwarts came. Liberalism and decentralization are generally favored by the westerly republics, Slovenia and Croatia, where living standards are twice as high as in Macedonia or Montenegro. They can then take advantage of their well-established industries, their more highly trained and skilled people, and their connections with the West to work for themselves instead of being heavily taxed and held back for the benefit of Bosnia or Macedonia. From the standpoint of the gross product and the average standard of living in the country as a whole, the argument makes sense, but that may be small consolation in the rest of the country. Serbia, the largest republic, stands somewhere in the middle in economic development and also in these controversies but tends to lean to the side of centralism for various reasons, including tradition and the fact that its capital, Belgrade, is also the capital of Yugoslavia.

Bakarić said early in 1966 that tension between nationalities was question number two in Yugoslavia, second to the economic reform; but if the battle for the reform and against bureaucratic centralism was not won, it could become question number one.[8] Greater tension could lead some republics to think of secession. While that would be a counsel of despair, it may be that a looser form of federalism, even confederation, would ultimately give the country the stability it needs.

### Socialist Self-Government and the Role of the Party

Parallel to the workers' councils in industry, the Yugoslav leadership introduced in the 1950s a reform of local government, to give the people a sense of greater participation in the political life of the country. The reform consisted in a revision and broadening of the functions of the "people's committees," which until then were little more than local instruments of the federal government in Belgrade. They were now tied in with the functions of the workers' councils, providing financial resources and mak-

8 *Borba*, March 6, 1966.

ing certain decisions on investment. They were also given new powers over the management of "nonproductive activities" such as schools and welfare services.

As with the workers' councils, the obvious question was how much of the new system was appearance and how much was reality. The same tests could be applied: Did all control lie with the party authorities in Belgrade and their agents, or could local interests and concerns, within or outside the party, make themselves heard? The results, as might be expected, have been mixed. The party's role has been strong, because political questions even on the local level are crucial to its ultimate authority. Despite the supposed limitation of the League of Communists to an "educational" role after the Sixth Congress in 1952, the change was not easily understood by local party representatives or apparent to the ordinary citizen.

Over the years, however, there has been a notable strengthening of the people's committees, which have now become communal assemblies under the constitution of 1963. They are recognized organs of government, not mere "front" organizations. They have their own sources of income. They exercise real powers over enterprises and public services. Inspired by local pride and pressures, they have often used those powers unwisely, but the important political fact is that they have used them at all.

The changing make-up of the organs of local government reflects a certain evolution toward more democratic forms. In the beginning the members of a people's committee were elected on the basis of a single list which, though it might contain some nonparty names, was drawn up by party authorities. Later, the selection process was broadened to allow the proposing and discussion of candidates at open meetings of the committees themselves, and to allow the voters a free choice between two candidates for some of the seats. In the elections of 1965 the number of candidates was roughly twice the number of seats at the communal level; the range of choice on the republic and federal levels was smaller, but there were some contests. An open political competition with full and free debate on major issues is still not possible, however. The League of Communists and the Socialist Alliance (the official mass organization) "help to a great extent to realize the full meaning of democracy in the nomination and electoral procedures," as an authoritative source puts it.[4]

The Tito regime has made this exercise of "social self-government" a central principle of its doctrine and its constitutional law. The commune, according to the constitution of 1963, is "the basic social-political community," and self-government by the citizens in the commune is "the political foundation of the uniform social-political system." Constitutional provisions are no sure guide to political practice, in Yugoslavia or anywhere else, but there is a sense of commitment here to a principle of self-government, hedged though it may be by the role of the party. The existing institutions by no means constitute a free and open system. A more pertinent question is whether they hold the possibility of extending the measure of free choice and free debate, the promise of a transition from one-party rule to something else. Such a development would be of very great significance for the world. History has recorded previous cases of dictatorial regimes gradually introducing representative institutions, but no instance of a Communist party giving up a monopoly of political power, despite official mythology about the party state becoming the state "of all the people" and eventually withering away when "full communism" is achieved.

The Yugoslav Communists have shown considerable interest in such theoretical questions. In the early years after the break with Stalin, when they were looking for ways to show how they were holding to true Marxism-Leninism while Stalin was ruling the Soviet Union by means of an Oriental, bureaucratic despotism, they began to talk about the withering away of state and party as socialism was consolidated and new kinds of relations among citizens were established. This line of thinking was put forward largely by Milovan Djilas, then the ideological spokesman of the regime in the polemic with Stalin. It found its way into the program adopted at the Sixth Party Congress in 1952 when the conflict was at its height. That program established a new role, and a new name, for the Communist Party of Yugoslavia. The main idea was that the new League of Communists should per-

[4] Mirko Bošković, "Elections in Yugoslavia," *Socialist Thought and Practice,* January-March 1965, pp. 93-101.

form an educational rather than a directing function. It should point the way, encourage officials and citizens to build socialism, and set a fine example, but not order, instruct, or use "administrative measures" (i.e., police terror and pressure) to bring the people into line.

In reality, the change was one of emphasis. The party did not cease to be in charge of all policy and its execution. The idea of its withering was quietly dropped after its main proponent, Djilas, carried his theories too far and was cast aside by the other leaders.

The Djilas affair, which became a personal matter between him and Tito with feelings of betrayal on both sides, is a story which need not be told here. Its origins lay in the thinking and temperament of Djilas himself. He took the arguments against Stalinism and especially the program of 1952 most seriously, and his thought went on from there. Yugoslavia, he believed, must proceed without delay to build the new humane and democratic socialist society of which its leaders talked. That meant that its progressive dynamism must be maintained and not allowed to degenerate through the establishment of a new class of privileged Communists. It meant also, since socialism had triumphed in Yugoslavia and was no longer in danger of challenge from the former bourgeois parties, that full play must be given to democratic principles and to the contention of ideas, something that could not be accomplished within the one-party system. In his later writings Djilas reached the conclusion that the socialist system as practised in Communist states did not and could not allow true freedom and provided no answer to man's needs. But his first proposition was challenge enough, for it would have denied to the Communist party its dominant role, throwing open political power to the contention of undetermined forces of popular will or opinion, something no Communist regime has ever done.

Understandably, Tito and the other leaders could not accept these arguments, and Djilas' disgrace was inevitable. It does not follow from that, however, that the Yugoslav leadership has maintained a rigid line, rejecting everything for which Djilas argued in the period from 1950 to 1954. On the contrary, it has proceeded on a flexible and experimental course over the years in developing political institutions, loosening bureaucratic procedures, cutting down the use of arbitrary force, and allowing greater freedom of expression. Kardelj stated in 1956 that the one-party system would develop not into a multi-party system but into a "non-party Socialist democracy,"[5] and this has been the official view ever since. Yugoslavia went farther than any socialist state, with the possible exception of Poland for a brief period after 1956, in tolerance of free discussion, in restraint in using the party apparatus to enforce uniformity, and in freeing scholarship of the bonds of doctrine and the party line. New conditions in recent years, and especially the constitution of 1963 and the reforms of 1965, have given further impetus to these political trends, not only in confirming the system of "social self-government" but also in expanding the independence of the judiciary, increasing the role of the federal and the republican legislatures, and in enhancing the still limited freedom of choice in the electoral process.

The big question remains: How far can these trends go without modifying the position of ultimate power now occupied by the party? The constitution begs the question by setting forth all the principles and rules on social self-government, compulsory rotation in office, and the like, at the same time confirming the role of the League of Communists as the "prime mover" of political activity. The system is carried on as if there were no contradiction. The party leadership remains in charge, and it is the party which pushes the new economic reforms. There is, however, a crystallization of thought at different poles within the party itself which throws doubt on the stability of the present balance. Some on the liberal side have begun to see the authority of the party, where it is exercised by "apparatchiks" with no special abilities and intent only on preservation of power in the old way, as an obstacle to the country's progress. Some on the side of traditional party discipline see the whole trend of liberalization beyond fixed points of control as a threat to the party itself and to the socialist system. These two sets of views are at the core of Yugoslav politics. And they are obviously pertinent to the ques-

[5] "Evolution in Yugoslavia," *Foreign Affairs,* July 1956, p. 593.

tion of what happens at the end of the Tito era. Even now, the party no longer controls every trend in Yugoslav society.

The Fourth Plenum of the Central Committee of the League of Communists held in June 1966, which ended with the stunning announcement of the ouster of Ranković from his party and governmental posts, may represent a watershed in Yugoslavia's development comparable to that of 1948. Whatever the validity of charges that he was engaged in a conspiracy, there is no doubt that he had built up an independent apparatus of power based on control of party cadres and on the security police. He was using that apparatus to invade the jurisdiction of other high officials (including the State Secretary for Foreign Affairs) and to seek key points of control in the government and in the party. It was apparently the "bugging" of Tito's own premises that blew the lid off. A carefully chosen party commission made a thorough investigation, and Ranković was through.

The significance of the affair lay not in the fact that Ranković was grasping for power, either to push Tito aside or to make sure of succeeding him in due time. As Vice President of the Republic, he was already Tito's logical successor as President and perhaps also as Secretary General of the Party. The real significance lay in the fact that Ranković had become the symbol of the old order, of "Stalinism" (the term used by Tito in his public statement announcing the party's decisions), of government by police methods, and of resistance to the new reforms. The struggle within the party had been going on since 1962. That Tito came to the point of firing "Comrade Marko," who had been with him through thick and thin since the early years of the movement, was a measure of how strong the current for reform had become and how much the party itself had changed.

After the fall of Ranković one could almost feel the atmosphere of relief and the gusts of fresh air blowing through public and party offices throughout Yugoslavia. Differences among party leaders over the pace and character of change remained, but there was an evident desire on all sides to cut down the size and the power of the security service and to clear away "bureaucratic" obstruction to the economic reforms. The affair had also thrown a new light on the nationality question in its relation to party leadership. Ranković and his cohorts were widely condemned for Serbian chauvinism, but no other important Serbian leaders were openly associated with him or with that charge. As the highest ranking Serb in the party, he had kept others from rising to top positions, and when the showdown came, the Serbs stood with the Croats, Slovenes and the rest in condemning him. But appearances could be deceptive. Neither Serbian nationalism nor party centralism had vanished from the political scene.

### The Succession and the Future

The reasons why Yugoslavia in the mid-1960s seemed to be in a state of simmering crisis, which burst through the surface with the Ranković case, lay in the coming together of three sets of circumstances. The first was a growing restlessness, evident in the change in generations and expressed in demands for freer expression, in criticism of the narrow outlook of the party authorities; in short, many of the intellectuals, and with them much of the youth, were ranging beyond the official philosophy and the party line. Second, economic problems created divisions in the party, as did the reforms which were adopted to provide an answer to them, and these differences were tied to conflicting views among regions and nationalities and to differences of outlook on foreign relations. Third was the fact that Marshal Tito was not immortal. The party and the country had to prepare for a succession, which would be made more difficult by the existence of opposing tendencies on matters vital to their future.

It was probably inevitable that the Communist party, trying to find its own way apart from Moscow after 1948, should try to find a *modus vivendi* with the people of Yugoslavia. Events since then have shown that it has done so, in a number of ways, although in one sector or another of society there has been plenty of discontent. The critics are looking for a future within an evolving system, not organizing opposition to the system itself. Such forces for change, however, are none the less significant for being evolutionary rather than revolutionary. They exist within the party as well as outside it—an important fact because if the party is going to undergo any fundamental change, it will probably be from within.

Wide-ranging criticism comes especially from the intellectual elite: philosophers, economists, teachers, writers. It is a well-known fact that the intelligentsia is not the source of political power in Communist states, and that much of the toughness and resilience of the League of Communists of Yugoslavia has rested on its use of the techniques of power on all levels, rather than its intellectual persuasiveness, despite its declared role of educator of the people. Nevertheless, one cannot discount the power of the intellectual elite in any of the countries of Eastern Europe. Through history, through a succession of regimes, they have held an influential position in society, often as forerunners of change.

Some of the philosophical and literary writing of recent years, especially in Slovenia and Croatia, cannot be taken as other than a challenge to the narrowness and timidity of the party leadership. Outspoken literary periodicals published in Ljubljana, largely under the inspiration of young writers and teachers, made so bold as to suggest a multiparty political system. Not surprisingly, they were suppressed. Yet other journals, especially *Praxis* of Zagreb and *Gledišta* of Belgrade, continued to publish critiques, largely from Marxist premises, of the policies and practices of party and government. Some of the arguments were answered in official publications. Others were ignored. The significant fact is that writers continue to probe into the nature of Yugoslav society and to discuss the institutions best suited to it. As a prominent philosopher wrote:

> The question of authority, even of supreme ideological authority, is today an open issue facing Marxist philosophy. For how—and this, after all, seems to be the crucial question, the answer to which is nearly always avoided—are we to develop Marxist thought at all . . . if we cannot, in principle, have different, even divergent, views on some issues from those held by the classics. . . ."[6]

In a way, such critics seem over-concerned with ideology, which they feel the party doctrinaires are trying to keep in a strait

[6] Danko Grlić in *Praxis*, February-March, 1964, p. 54.

jacket in seeking a consistency which Yugoslav practice has already gone beyond. Their free-wheeling criticism has alienated some of the "liberals" in positions of responsibilty in party and governmental positions as well as the "dogmatic" types. Yet its significance as a symbol of the new generation's impatience with official limitations on thought and its tendency to question the philosophic basis of the existing order remains profound. The party leaders, especially Tito, react against it, yet the party itself is not tied to any static doctrine and is opening up new lines of experimentation and inquiry. And there is no denying that the pursuit of material goods is becoming much more real, to most party members and others alike, than exercises in theory.

The now famous articles of Mihajlo Mihajlov, a Yugoslav writer and lecturer of Russian descent, provide another example both of the spirit of the intellectuals and of the dilemma of the regime in dealing with them. It would be a mistake to exaggerate the importance of the Mihajlov affair, for he was something of a lone wolf, seemed especially interested in promoting himself, and openly tried to mobilize pressure from abroad to support his case against his own government. Nevertheless, his "Moscow Summer" articles appearing in *Delo,* an account of his impressions of the Soviet scene which started it all, and his later statements did raise questions about literary and political freedom which were relevant to Yugoslavia as well as to the Soviet Union.

Although it was Moscow's angry demands which spurred the Yugoslav government into banning the offending articles, what raised the incident to the status of an affair of state was a personal intervention by President Tito, who rebuked a delegation of public prosecutors for not having taken immediate action against "this reactionary." Mentioning "distorted concepts" which had appeared in other periodicals, he said he had to ask himself "whether this is not some sort of organization." The "tendency which we at one time described as Djilasism" seemed to be appearing in a new form. This obviously could not be tolerated.[7] Needless to say, legal action was then taken. The President showed himself to be extraordinarily sensitive, both on

[7] Statement of February 11, 1965, published in *Kommunist,* March 4, 1965, and in *Borba,* same date.

the score of the challenge to his domestic system and on that of his relations with Moscow. There was a certain parallel with the earlier outbursts and actions against Djilas, which came at times when Tito was trying to improve relations with the Soviet Union.

Like Djilas, whom he admires, Mihajlov later spoke out against the one-party system. He tried to establish an opposition periodical, thus inviting a new prosecution as he was then under a suspended sentence for his first transgression. The Yugoslav government was obviously desirous of ridding itself of the embarrassment of the case rather than with building it up further. But Mihajlov was not cooperative and was again convicted and imprisoned.[8] In handling other dissident writers, including Miodrag Bulatović, whose early novels won critical acclaim in translation outside the country, the regime has chosen to shrug off their criticism as of no consequence.

The regime's running controversy with the intellectuals, both inside and outside the party, illustrates some of its basic dilemmas. It wants to carry out reforms which will improve the economy and to win the voluntary collaboration of the people in making the political and the economic system work. The leaders want as broad a base as possible in the population, especially among the intellectuals and the youth, for building their socialist "great society." Yet their ambivalence in dealing with new and nonconformist ideas leaves open the question whether they will accommodate themselves to the trend for broader and more rapid evolution and reform, or whether they will resist it as too dangerous. Tito himself has been a model of ambivalence. Early in 1963 he made several tough speeches against the "small number of barren intellectuals . . . who hover on the outside of our socialist reality," the "carriers of negative influences from abroad."[9] He said that as head of the party he had to take

[8] For an account of the Mihajlov affair, see Stevan K. Pavlowitch, "Mihajlo Mihajlov and the Revolt of the Intellectuals," *Review* (London), no. 5, 1965, pp. 309-327. An English translation of *Moscow Summer*, including the third installment which never appeared in Yugoslavia, was published by Farrar, Straus and Giroux (New York, 1965).

[9] See especially his speech to the People's Youth Congress, printed in *Borba*, January 24, 1963.

responsibility for culture, as he did for industry and agriculture, and to decide what was good and what was bad, what was permissible and what was not. In February 1966 he repeated the familiar theme that freedom to spread decadent and anti-socialist influences from abroad was not the kind of freedom that could be tolerated in Yugoslavia. He deplored the petty bourgeois talk of the cafés and complained that it was difficult to distinguish the voice of the party from the voice of the streets.[10]

The various Communist party leaders and members do not all react in the same way. As in economic matters, there are those who tend to be reformist and others who tend to be conservative. The latter, many of them old-time partisans, are suspicious of change and of the free expression of ideas as dangerous to the party's authority. The former, including many of the young intellectuals, want to open the windows and let in some fresh air. These are not definable factions so much as general tendencies which exist within the ranks of the party and sometimes within the minds and hearts of individual members. The momentum is on the side of those seeking a new assessment of the party's role, which may mark a break with Leninism as portentous as the earlier repudiation of Stalinism.

The Fifth Plenum of the Central Committee decided, in October 1966, to reorganize the League of Communists at the top, making Tito President instead of Secretary General, creating an enlarged Presidium, giving Mijalko Todorović, a Serb, the new post of Secretary of the Executive Committee, and initiating a full-scale reassessment of the role of the party in the political and social structure. That reassessment has already called into question the classic formula of democratic centralism on the ground that in practice in all socialist states there has been too much centralism and not enough democracy. It is therefore necessary "to break the long monopoly held by small groups of men at the highest level . . ."[11] The party must be not only reformed but transformed.

There is a new class in Yugoslavia. It is not Djilas' "new class"

---

[10] Address to the Third Plenum of the Central Committee of the League of Communists, February 25, 1966 (*Borba*, February 26, 1966).
[11] Krste Crvenkovski, interview in *Politika*, October 23, 1966.

of privileged party functionaries but a whole new group of professional and managerial men and women of the postwar generation. They are sure to put their stamp on the country's future, and they do not find Tito's appeals for a renewal of the old party spirit a totally adequate answer. As Kardelj said after the fall of Ranković, the discussion is only beginning.

As long as Tito is at the apex, there will probably be no major convulsion or showdown. He is not a figurehead president, withdrawn from the rough and tumble of politics, as he seemingly wished to be a few years ago. While no longer possessing total authority, he has the prestige to keep the others in line and to continue to get the general support of the people. Such a position of great personal prestige and authority, however, with its international as well as domestic aspects, cannot be passed on intact to a successor. That is especially true in Yugoslavia, where the ruling group has no one who could hope to play the same role. Therefore, some contention among conflicting trends, views, and personalities seems likely, no matter how much preparation is made to avert it. Tito has been most concerned with keeping party and country together in the face of tension among factions and nationalities. His decision not to prosecute Ranković was followed, in December 1966, by the release of Djilas. The latter act balanced the former; together, they constituted an effort to clear the books of past controversies, personal and political, and establish harmony as Tito approached the end of his reign.

Succession to the presidency of the Republic seemed very much unsettled following the ouster of Ranković from the post of vice-president. His successor, Koča Popović, is by no means assured of the top job, which requires election by the Federal Assembly. The presidency, moreover, might not be the most powerful post, for Tito holds also the position of President of the League of Communists, and no one has been designated, at least not publicly, to take over that job. Edvard Kardelj, who is President of the Federal Assembly and a loyal associate of Tito over the years, would be a natural choice, but he has never won great popularity. In the public eye he is still a schoolmaster and philosopher rather than a dynamic leader, and as a Slovene he is a member of a small nationality. Although he has deplored the tendency to use the labels of "conservative" and "liberal" or "progressive," the fact is that both he and Vladimir Bakarić, the leading Croatian Communist, represent the liberal trend likely to gain momentum in the future. There may be others to be heard from. The party leadership, particularly the Serbian element, contains a number of ambitious men. The Minister of Defense, Ivan Goš-njak, a Croat loyal only to Tito, is not a political leader; but in the event of a struggle for power the role of the army might be decisive.

Whatever the personalities, the succession is bound to bring into sharper relief some of the differences and contradictions which are already visible above the surface of Yugoslav politics. The disappearance of Ranković, who was clearly Moscow's favorite, seemed to remove the question of succession, partially at least, from considerations of foreign policy. No Serbian leader could turn wholly to the side of the conservative "apparatchiks," abandon the economic reforms, or turn his back on the West. Any regime will depend on Croatia and Slovenia to pursue a successful economic policy. The party leaders from those republics will have very substantial bargaining power, although they could not run the country without the cooperation of the powerful Serbian element. There will be questions that will have to be settled by compromise within the party, between wings of the party, and perhaps between the party and the people. If they are not, they will demand settlement outside the party.

The succession to Tito may be managed quite smoothly. The existing constitution makes that possible on the governmental side, though it does not cover the party side. But the underlying questions which have troubled Yugoslavia in the age of Tito will not disappear. They may be more difficult to cope with when his authority is no longer there. It seems a reasonable conclusion that they must be dealt with in ways that gain the necessary minimum of popular acceptance in all parts of the country if a grave crisis comparable to that of the prewar period, which prepared the way for the destruction of the Yugoslav state, is to be avoided.

## Chapter IX

# Yugoslavia and the West

Policy toward Yugoslavia ought to be lifted out of the old arguments and disputes which have swirled about it in the past. Nothing is gained by putting a label on that country—Communist or neutralist or nationalist—and then reaching conclusions from too narrow, or too broad, a premise. Nor by keeping the discussion so closely confined within the framework of foreign aid as it has been in the past, so that all issues come down to whether it is politic or proper or moral to give American taxpayers' money to Marshal Tito.

That Yugoslavia is run by a Communist regime cannot be denied. That the regime is deliberately participating in an international Communist conspiracy against the United States and the Western world can be denied. All the evidence is against it. For Yugoslav Communists, it is an article of faith that capitalism will be superseded by socialism everywhere, just as most Americans choose to believe that freedom will win out over those who suppress it. "Socialism" remains a holy word, and whatever the Yugoslav leaders do they do in its name. It is still relevant, in some respects, to Yugoslavia's relations with other states, but we need not be over-concerned with Marxist theology or ritual bearing no relationship to policy and action. If Belgrade's position on some international issues is parallel to that of Moscow, it is necessary in each case to look at the causes and the consequences.

Nonalignment, more than socialism, is put forward as a guiding principle of Yugoslav foreign policy. As a logical result of the country's having left one bloc without joining the other, it once was such a principle. But the range of relationships with both East and West has been so varied and complex, becoming more so as the cold war has slackened, that it is no longer a particularly useful term. It is less a question of how to stay unengaged than of what kind of engagements, in each direction, short of alliance or exclusive alignment, are in the national interest. Nor does solidarity with the nonaligned of Asia and Africa, exhilarating as this leap into global politics has been, provide more than a limited explanation of Yugoslavia's policies or answer to its problems.

Nationalism explains a great deal in the recent history of Central and Eastern Europe, especially in Yugoslavia's relations with Russia, with Germany, and with its neighbors. But Yugoslav nationalism, other than in a clear case of united resistance to outside pressure, rests on the uncertain base of a delicate balance of coexistence among its own national groups. These differences definitely affect Yugoslav foreign policy although they by no means determine it. Yugoslavia has interests common to all its nationalities, and they lie closer to home than Asia, Africa, and Latin America. Its world role, significant as it has been, should not blind us to the fact that in the long run the Yugoslavs, leaders and people, will have to find their destiny in Europe.

### The Relationship with Moscow

The nerve center of Yugoslav foreign policy is what a keen observer has called the love-hate complex toward "the state that is simultaneously the fatherland of the Revolution, Mother Russia, and the intolerable oppressor of East European nations."[1] It goes well back in South Slav history, where the themes of national identity, liberation, and Slavdom are tangled together. The addition of the Communist dimension, with the advent of national leaders whose early training and inspiration came from

[1] Dennison I. Rusinow, "Yugoslavia Reaps the Harvest of Coexistence," *American Universities Field Staff Reports*, vol. XI, no. 1 (Yugoslavia), January 1964, p. 3.

Soviet Russia and who believed in "the revolution," made the psychological aspects of Yugoslav attitudes and policies all the sharper, but no easier to define or to predict. Fear of domination by Moscow has alternated with a yearning for acceptance by Moscow. Status in the "international workers' movement" has a special lure, but to let Moscow determine the nature of that status becomes insupportable. The experience with Stalin seared itself into the souls of the Yugoslav leaders. We can dismiss the idea that Yugoslavia will ever accept a satellite relationship to the Soviet Union. But that conclusion does not entirely dispose of the question whether Yugoslavia, with all its reservations with respect to the sovereignty and equality of independent socialist nations, will work together with the Soviet Union for the advance of Soviet power and the victory of "socialism" over the "capitalist" West.

It is a point, already discussed at some length in preceding chapters, which may be given clarification and emphasis by an attempt to answer, in summary form, three critical questions:

1. What kind of association with the Soviet Union does Yugoslavia seek?
2. What is the Yugoslav interpretation of the evolution and policies of the Soviet Union since the death of Stalin?
3. What is the Yugoslav concept of an international order in which Yugoslavia's interests and the general cause of socialism can best be advanced?

The first question finds its answer in the whole record of Yugoslav policy since 1948. Independence is the consistent thread running through all its phases. Yugoslavia could accept the authority of no other state or party. It could accept no Comintern or Cominform, no organization which purported to set the line for all Communist states and parties to follow. It would not join in conferences and declarations by which the Soviet leadership, as in 1957, 1960 and 1965, tried to get other Communist parties to adopt a common line. In addition, Yugoslavia's choice of non-alignment at the time of the reconciliation with Moscow meant that it would avoid all ties of alliance with the Soviet Union, even though such a relationship would have meant no loss of sovereignty or independence in the legal sense. It did not join the Warsaw Pact. And it has avoided any economic ties with the East which might have moved outside its national frontiers the basic powers of decision affecting its own economy.

Tito never left any doubt, however, even in the time of his struggle with Stalin, that he did not wish to see Yugoslavia cut off from the community of socialist states. He never let his growing ties with the West close the doors to forging a new basis for relations with the Soviet Union and Eastern Europe. Indeed, he used his relations with the West and with the third world as levers to help move the Soviet leadership in that direction. How far has it moved from insistence on dominance to acceptance of equality? Or, more to the point, how far do the Yugoslavs think it has moved?

Some observers, tracing Tito's course from the first reconciliation with Khrushchev through the renewal of party contacts, the Yugoslav stand on the Hungarian revolt of 1956, the soft-pedaling of the renewed dispute over "revisionism" in 1957-60, and the steady march toward parallel policies since 1961, have concluded that he has in fact lost his potential for disruption and gone all the way back to a common line with Moscow; that though the label of independence may still be displayed and the "camp" may have changed its character, they are working together in a common cause, with the strategy inevitably determined by the larger and stronger partner. Such conclusions come not only from those addicted to simple interpretations—as that a Communist leader is by definition engaged in the world Communist conspiracy to conquer the world—but also from informed scholars and journalists who cite public speeches and actions to support their thesis.[2]

This is the gravamen of the second question posed above. Have Soviet policies so changed since Stalin's death that Yugoslavia can wholeheartedly support them? The Yugoslav Commu-

[2] See especially Milorad Drachkovitch, "The Soviet-Yugoslav Relationship," *Orbis*, Winter 1962, pp. 437-452; Viktor Meier, "Yugoslav Communism," in William E. Griffith, ed., *Communism in Europe: Continuity, Change, and the Sino-Soviet Dispute*, Vol. I (Cambridge, M.I.T. Press, 1964), pp. 19-84; J. F. Brown, *The New Eastern Europe: The Khrushchev Era and After* (New York: Frederick A. Praeger, 1966), pp. 178-181.

nists, while maintaining certain reservations, see a great transformation both in the Soviet Union itself and in the structure of the Communist world. The objective fact of change is undeniable, and the directions it has taken have been those advocated by the Yugoslavs. It is not that Nikita Khrushchev and his successors have been convinced by Yugoslav arguments. They were forced into new policies by the pressures they have been up against both at home and abroad. They made concessions to their own people because they had to. They failed to maintain Stalin's empire in Eastern Europe because they discovered it could not be done. They adopted the line of coexistence in foreign policy because the high tension of the cold war was becoming dangerous and damaging to Soviet interests, and they saw that new methods could serve them better.

The Yugoslav Communist leaders, like most Marxists, believe in the inexorable march of history, especially along the lines of their own development. They find plenty of evidence to confirm the theory that other socialist states will in general follow those lines, if not in their domestic political structures where each has its own special conditions, then in the relationships among them and with the non-Communist world. If the key word in domestic developments was liberalization or de-Stalinization, in relations with Communist states it was equality, and in relations with the West it was coexistence. These words describe what had been taking place in Yugoslav policy and what the Yugoslavs saw happening, at a slower pace and with differences in conditions, in the Soviet Union.

There is much to be said for the above argument, even if it does outrun the facts. The Soviet Union has adopted certain new tactics in dealing with the West. It has come, or been brought, into a new relationship with its former satellites in Eastern Europe, although it still has powerful instruments of control, including the ultimate sanction of military force. The Yugoslavs applaud and encourage these trends, but with the caution not to join the club or to risk their own hard-won independence.

It is good to have more solidarity among socialist states, the Yugoslav Communists believe, so long as it is voluntary. But for what purpose? Not for conducting a military or cold-war offensive against the West. Not for isolating the "socialist" part of the world as an integrated bloc cut off from other countries. To answer the third question posed above, it is fundamental to the Yugoslav view that while ideology may color relations among states with elements of affinity or of antagonism, the international order of which they all are a part must rest on certain universal and generally accepted principles which are stated in the United Nations Charter: avoidance of aggression and the use of force, nonintervention in the affairs of other states, self-determination of nations, peaceful settlement of disputes. Thus, socialism cannot be forcibly imposed by socialist states on nonsocialist states any more than a certain type of socialism can be imposed by one socialist state on another. Socialism will make its way in all countries of the world, says the program of the League of Communists, in accordance with the specific conditions and national character in each case. Meanwhile, no country can build socialism or anything else if it is engulfed by war or torn by a cold-war conflict between capitalist and socialist states. Hence the absolute necessity of peaceful coexistence.

As the Yugoslav Communist leaders see it, peaceful coexistence is the only sane policy for Yugoslavia, a small country which has nothing to gain and everything to lose by conflict with neighboring states or with larger powers. They have a genuine interest in seeing relations between the great powers develop on a basis of coexistence and negotiated settlements rather than of tension and trials of force. Yugoslavia will want to maintain solidarity with other socialist states, but only in the pattern of its own coexistence, and theirs too, with the West.

As the Afro-Asian dimension of Yugoslav policy has receded, the European aspect has become more prominent. At the U.N. General Assembly of 1965, Rumania suggested that a group of European states, both aligned and neutral, seek common ground in order to promote peaceful coexistence and security in Europe. The Assembly unanimously adopted a resolution generally recommending more contacts, improved relations, and an atmosphere of confidence among European states.[3] The states which sponsored the resolution (Belgium, Denmark, Sweden, Finland,

[3] Resolution 2129 (XX), December 21, 1965.

Austria, Yugoslavia, Hungary, Rumania, and Bulgaria) then set about carrying it forward. In September 1966, representatives of their parliaments met at Belgrade, the Yugoslavs serving as genial and enthusiastic hosts. Their diplomats met again at the 1966 session of the U.N. General Assembly. One cannot predict results, but this is a sign of the times. The East European states may try to use it to advance the Soviet purpose of isolating West Germany and excluding the United States from Europe, but the others, including Yugoslavia, can be counted on to resist such an attempt. The influence of Yugoslavia, like that of other small states on both sides, is likely to be thrown on the side of a European settlement which appears to safeguard their own security; and they will try to push the great powers in that direction.

### Yugoslavia and European Security

Western observers may be pardoned a certain skepticism toward Yugoslav interpretations of Soviet and Western policies. As we have seen, gratification over the shift from Stalinism to Khrushchevism may have induced some wishful thinking in Belgrade with respect to a basic change in Soviet aims, or at least suggested the tactical advantages of assuming this to be so. At any rate, whether from conviction or by political design, Yugoslav public utterances have pictured the "peaceful coexistence" line of the Soviet Union, like their own, as genuinely aimed at peace and stability in Europe. But there is a difference between coexistence as the strategy of a great power trying to increase its scope for maneuver, to weaken its major adversary, and to carry on a "struggle," and coexistence simply as a means of reducing tension and the risks of war; there is a further difference between these versions and the idea of coexistence as a policy aimed at seeking compromise settlements of outstanding issues.[4] The Yugoslav Communists have surely been aware of these distinctions. They chose to interpret the Soviet line as parallel to their own, perhaps with the idea of helping to make it so. Accordingly, while they

[4] See Marshall D. Shulman, *Beyond the Cold War* (New Haven: Yale University Press, 1966), pp. 53-58.

did not back the Soviet purposes of dividing and weakening the West, they endorsed many of the specific positions which the Soviet Union had adopted for the achievement of those purposes.

Yugoslavia has taken the position that, since Soviet power is not a threat, NATO as an alliance with aggressive tendencies and an anti-Communist background ought to be disbanded. The Warsaw Pact could then also be dissolved. Yugoslavia supports Poland and the Soviet Union on the question of the Oder-Neisse frontier, and on the desirability of disengagement on the lines of the Rapacki Plan. It opposes German access, under any guise, to nuclear weapons. It supports the Soviet position that the existence of the two Germanys is a reality that should be accepted, and that they can work out their problem between themselves. It maintains diplomatic relations with East Germany, which it first recognized in 1957 and as a sequel found its relations with the German Federal Republic broken by a swift reaction on the part of the latter to uphold the Hallstein doctrine. None of these positions squares with those of the United States.

What the Yugoslavs see as the way to peace and security in Europe is to stabilize the existing situation and take the tension out of it, preferably by East-West agreement. To the extent that the Soviet Union is a *status quo* power, they support the Soviet line. To the extent that the West wants a change, they oppose the West. They are not interested in the reunification of Germany. Nor do they wish to see Western influence supplant Soviet influence in the states of Eastern Europe now associated with the Soviet Union in the Warsaw Pact. These are also the immediate aims of Soviet policy in Europe: to keep Germany, and Europe, divided, and to secure general acceptance of the legitimacy of Ulbricht's regime in East Germany and the Communist regimes in Eastern Europe.

The Western nations have their differences in judging the nature and magnitude of the Soviet threat. With the possible exception of France, however, they put no faith in the theory that their alliance is no longer essential to security. Aside from its importance as a deterrent to war, Western power, organized in NATO, remains necessary to maintain a balance without which an acceptable political settlement could not be reached. Nor do the Western nations, including France, accept the argument that durable peace can be built on the denial of unity to the German nation and the persistence of Soviet power as the dominant force in Eastern Europe. Before concluding that Yugoslav policy is Soviet policy and hostile to the West, however, it is necessary to look a little more closely at Yugoslav interests and aims with respect to these two points.

So far as Germany is concerned, Yugoslavia's position is marginal rather than direct. Its people have bitter memories of the war, but they are not vitally involved in the German question as the Poles and the Czechs are. Yugoslavia has no disputed borders with Germany. Despite some unsolved differences (reparation for war damage, for example) and a propensity to strong statements about West German militarism and revanchism, it carries on beneficial commercial relations with Bonn despite the absence of diplomatic missions. Regardless of asseverations of friendship with Pankow, Yugoslav Communists have no respect for Herr Ulbricht and no stake in the maintenance of his regime except that it bears a socialist label. They fear a reunification of Germany through the absorption of the eastern zone by the Federal Republic, for that might be such a shock that it would shake every Communist regime in Europe, and such a shift in the international balance that it would bring on a major war. But if German unity could be negotiated, with safeguards against those eventualities, it might well be acceptable. On the other hand, Yugoslavia has no reason to favor, and every reason to fear, an outcome which would bring all of Germany under Soviet control, for that would mean a Soviet-dominated Europe, probably a world war, and almost certainly the end of Yugoslav independence.

The question of German reunification is one which may eventually be settled only by East-West agreement or by a slow evolution to the point where the Soviet Union is prepared to let it happen by action of the Germans themselves. Yugoslavia, with its independent policy, favors both negotiation toward an East-West settlement and evolution toward an atmosphere of détente. That is no contradiction of American, German, or European interests.

As for the future of Eastern Europe, if Yugoslavia stands for the *status quo* in the sense of wanting no entry of Western power into the region, it is no advocate of the *status quo* in the relations between the East European states and the Soviet Union. The whole thrust of its policy is to enlarge the opportunities for Rumania, Hungary and the others to have the independence now enjoyed by Yugoslavia. That, again, represents no contradiction of American and European interests.

### Yugoslavia's Own Interests

In the long run Yugoslav foreign policy cannot rest on floating abstractions or even on the bias or complexes of individual leaders. It is tied to the country's political and economic conditions, to internal forces arising from its own problems, and to the need for coping with the inevitable pulls and pressures exerted by stronger powers. Yugoslavia needs both the East and the West in its trade and other economic relations. It has needed each, at one time or another, to counter what it regarded as undue pressure from the other and to avoid the hazards of an exclusive relationship. In some ways the Yugoslavs have benefited from the cold war, getting assistance from both sides. But their desire to see it give way to a situation of greater stability in Europe is none the less genuine.

On the economic side, Yugoslavia's more important ties are with the Western nations. The West has been the source of essential credits. It produces what Yugoslavia needs to import. It has the markets where Yugoslavia can earn hard currencies. The world economy, not the Soviet bloc, offers the international division of labor in which the Yugoslav economy can find its place. The Western European countries, not the Soviet Union or Eastern Europe, provide large numbers of Yugoslav workers with jobs and training.[5] The West has the advanced technology. Reform of customs duties, devaluation of the dinar, membership in the

[5] At the beginning of 1966, an estimated 220,000 Yugoslav citizens were working in Western European countries, the greatest number of them in West Germany. This voluntary migration of workers, including some skilled experts, beginning about 1962, is viewed with mixed feelings by the Yugoslav government. It is tolerated, however, and even facilitated by agreements with Western governments. Although it represents a confession of economic weakness by a socialist state, it has the advantage of relieving the pressure of

General Agreement on Tariffs and Trade, and the whole series of economic reforms undertaken by Yugoslavia in the past few years fortify this tendency of economic association with the West and the world trading system. It is a turn to the West of enormous potential significance, although Yugoslav public statements do not say so. Trade with the East has recently jumped (to roughly 35 per cent of total trade in 1965), but primarily for the reason that a weak position in foreign exchange did not leave much choice. The decision does not lie in Belgrade alone. If the Western nations want Yugoslavia to look in their direction rather than eastward, they will have to do something about the obstacles that stand in the way.

On the political side, the Yugoslav leaders have now had years of experience, in differing circumstances, in dealing with Western nations. While some of them, including Tito, have shown a fear and concern over subversive bourgeois influences, they have seen that Western governments will deal with Yugoslavia on a normal basis and without pressure, allowing it to work out its own institutions. Experience has shown that coexistence between their kind of socialist regime and Western nations with various political and social systems can be a reality useful to both sides and not a mere cover for tactical maneuvers in the cold war.

Of all the Communist countries, Yugoslavia is the one which has developed the most normal relations with the West, has been the most aloof from alignments serving Soviet strategy against the West, and has been the most hostile to Communist China. It is the only one which has worked closely with the OEEC and its successor, OECD. In the United Nations and the specialized international agencies it has been the most cooperative in constructive international efforts in peacekeeping and economic development. Internally, it is the Communist state which has introduced the most drastic modifications of the totalitarian system through new institutions, recognition of the rights of the individual, and tolerance of dissent.

The West, in the way in which it deals with Yugoslavia, has

unemployment and adding to the country's supply of foreign exchange. Whether these workers will come home again is an open question. See Večeslav Holjevac, "New Economic Emigration," *Review of International Affairs*, April 5, 20, 1966; *Politika*, January 30, 1966; *Borba*, February 5, 1966.

the opportunity not only to encourage these trends and to strengthen that country's independence, but also to show other East European states the benefits to be reaped from an independent position. Rumania's evolution is a case in point; there should be others. But if the West shows that there is no place for Yugoslavia in the future envisioned for Europe, fails to take account of its special situation, and drives it toward dependence on the Soviet Union, then the other East European states will see no hope or advantage in trying to move toward a similar status.

A trend in Eastern Europe toward independence and reform and better relations with the West will make it more difficult for the Soviet Union to harness those countries to an anti-Western strategy. It could also have an effect within the Soviet Union itself. The pressures for change and reform exist there as well. The people of the Soviet Union know what is going on in Eastern Europe, especially those who may be in key positions in intellectual and scientific circles and in the management of the economy. The Soviet Union is not immune to the troubles which have led to the rash of experimentation and reforms in those countries. All have the problem of containing within a rigid political system the economic demands of an ever more complex society and the aspirations and ambitions of a restless and increasingly well-educated population. The trend, together with the Chinese challenge, seems already to have contributed to Soviet attitudes and policies toward the West which are more circumspect, less shrill in expression, less adventurous in action, more inclined toward détente. No firm conclusions can or should be drawn from what has happened thus far, but the trend is encouraging, and there is no denying that Yugoslavia and Eastern Europe have had something to do with it.

Mihajlo Mihajlov has made the striking statement that the struggle for economic reform, for intellectual freedom, and for a "democratic socialism" in Yugoslavia is crucial to the whole future development of the entire socialist bloc and to the struggle for "tomorrow's free humanity."[6] With characteristic Yugoslav overstatement he claims too much for his own country and for his

[6] Mihajlo Mihajlov, "Why We Are Silent," *New Leader*, August 30, 1965, pp. 12-15.

own view of the world. He is referring, moreover, not so much to the reforms and policies now in being as to those which are still necessary to end the Communists' monopoly of power and put life into the fine phrases of the constitution. His remark, nevertheless, gives perspective to the opportunities that may lie in the West's policies toward Yugoslavia. The last thing that should motivate those policies is a fear of communism in its Yugoslav form. Its greater threat, as the process of change goes on, should be to any leaders and governments who may still dream of harnessing world communism as an aggregate of power to overwhelm and destroy the citadels of the free world.

### Conclusions

In the light of all these factors, the interest of the United States seems clear. It is to strengthen the ties between Yugoslavia and the West. Developments within Yugoslavia confirm that conclusion. When Tito and Stalin quarreled, the United States wisely helped Yugoslavia. Wisely, too, it refrained from trying to exploit Tito's desperate position in meeting Stalin's assault to force changes in Yugoslavia's political system or to dominate its foreign policy. One reason for that decision was that pressure would not work, and that to try it would jeopardize immediate and more important aims. A second reason was the conviction that over the years the force of events would open Yugoslavia's doors and would bring in Yugoslavia itself changes on the domestic scene beneficial to the people and their relations with the West. This has happened to a perceptible degree, despite occasional cries of alarm from high-ranking Communists against the dangers of bourgeois influence. It is likely to continue. The expansion of educational and cultural cooperation could help it along tremendously.

Such considerations have given a substance to American policy toward Yugoslavia beyond the immediate motives of strategy and cold-war politics that brought the West to Tito's aid after 1948. The reality of national communism in Yugoslavia, plus the doctrine of "separate roads" for which Tito stood, meant the end of the united Communist world. The Soviet-Chinese break was far weightier in its effects, but Yugoslavia had the distinction of coming first, and it always retained a special importance because of its place in Europe and its proximity to the European members of the Soviet bloc. Furthermore, in charting its own course apart from Moscow, Yugoslavia has moved toward accommodation and good relations with the West, while China's independent course has been more hostile and intransigent than ever. If we are interested in the character and quality of the differences between Communist states, as we should be, then Yugoslavia deserves a closer look. For here there is something more than a difference in views on how to bury the capitalist world the more expeditiously. Here are trends which could put the issues between the Communist and non-Communist states, if not on the road to a settlement, at least into a quite different and more favorable perspective than they have been since the cold war began.

Because such considerations have not been understood, or have been rejected as the product of soft thinking, American policy toward Yugoslavia has been plagued by vexing controversies, both inside this country and in relations with the Yugoslavs, centering on the question of aid. It was doubtless an occasion for relief on the part of both governments when Presidents Kennedy and Tito could announce, after their meeting in October 1963, that American grant aid was no longer needed by Yugoslavia. Relations have been somewhat smoother since that time. The mere falling off of rancorous congressional debate on the annual aid bills, however, is no adequate substitute for a sounder understanding of the basis for policy.

By 1963 the time for major grant assistance was over and had been over for some years. But that was no reason to put development loans or surplus food sales for local currency or dollar credits beyond the pale—which the Congress has since done—and thus to deny to the United States government the capacity to act in its own interest. One can cite cases other than that of Yugoslavia to show the folly of our government's depriving itself of a useful instrument of policy, often the only one which can be effective in a given situation. As far as the Yugoslav case is concerned, the United States needs the flexibility to extend economic aid in specific situations or emergencies which may arise, such as a food shortage. Its continuing interest in Yugoslavia also dictates keeping the door open for the extension of loans by the U.S. government, international lending institutions, and private banks or companies. There is good reason, also, to permit the Yugoslavs to purchase military equipment and spare parts from the United States, as they have wished to do. Purchases from the Soviet Union are virtually their only alternative.

More important than aid in the long run is trade. If we want Yugoslavia to look westward, it has to be able to trade with the West. The attempt of the Congress in 1962 to legislate the end of most-favored-nation treatment as a punitive measure directed against communism was a mistake. It is advantageous for the whole Western relationship with Yugoslavia and the Communist countries that 50 per cent or more of Yugoslav trade is with Western Europe and North America. The Yugoslavs want to build up their markets in the West, so that they can purchase the goods they need. They want to participate in world trade and are opening up their own economy to the cold winds of international competition. They have no desire to be caught in the toils of a "socialist economic community" organized through the CMEA. They want to reach arrangements with the European Economic Community and with the European Free Trade Association. All they need is a chance to make their way. In its most concrete form, that means a chance to develop a thriving trade with the countries of the EEC, their biggest potential market, even as the latter moves toward greater integration. The political advantages, for the West as well as for Yugoslavia, are likely to outweigh the disadvantage to the economic interest of any Western state.

All these arguments may be logical. Yet the fact, already noted several times, is that they have not been convincing to all in the West, and especially to many members of the United States Congress. There the debate has often been between all-out opponents of aid, trade, or normal relations with any Communist country and apologetic supporters of the administration's requests bent on proving that they, too, dislike Tito and are alert to the dangers of being deceived by him. It is only too plain that the administration has not adequately explained its case to the public. In fact, the administration has not tried very hard to do so.

A big difficulty has been the limited scope of the debate, which frequently revolves round such questions as whether Tito is dependable, whether he will be on our side when the chips are down, whether it is morally or politically right to give aid to a Communist dictator, or whether Yugoslavia is taking part in some world Communist conspiracy. These are not the relevant questions today, if they ever were. The time has come to put policy toward Yugoslavia in the framework of a policy for Europe. The United States and its Western allies must find a general strategy for associating Eastern Europe with the growing European community. Such a strategy cannot be outlined in any precise form here. President de Gaulle is making his own, which includes increased diplomatic and cultural activity in Eastern Europe (including Yugoslavia), a dialogue with Moscow, and vague talk about building a Europe "from the Atlantic to the Urals." It includes also the dismantling of NATO. If he has annoyed and distressed other members of that organization, he has also compelled them to search more vigorously for sound alternatives of their own.

It does not follow that if building up the strength of the Western alliance has not brought an acceptable settlement in Central and Eastern Europe, weakening the West will lead to such a settlement. It does not follow, either, that nothing can be done about Eastern Europe until Western Europe has completed its own economic and political unity. It is perfectly possible, and eminently sensible, to attempt to maintain the strength and solidarity of the West while pursuing détente with the East. The West, unless its nations play into the hands of a Soviet strategy aimed at its division, has a favorable bargaining position thanks to its economic growth and to the troubles which have beset the Soviet bloc. It can use that power not to impose a settlement on the Soviet Union but to create a Europe toward which the East European states will be drawn by their own interests, by their economic needs, by their desire for greater independence, and by the inclinations of their own peoples. This is the great opportunity presented by the transformation which Eastern Europe, and even the Soviet Union to a lesser degree, has been undergoing. It is no quick process. The important point is to recognize the direction and to take account of it in the West's own policies. President Johnson's speech of October 7, 1966, on approaches to Eastern Europe was notable for showing official awareness of it.

How is Europe, the big Europe, to be made? How can a framework be found which provides an alternative to the present cold-war partition but avoids the anarchy of uncontrolled nationalism?[7] Blueprints are not particularly useful at this stage. Even the critical question of whether Western plans and policies for drawing the East European states into a new Europe should differentiate sharply between them and the Soviet Union, or include the latter as an indispensable element in the general scheme of "bridge-building," need not be given an immediate and final answer. Three main lines of thought and action seem indicated now. The first is, in the pursuit of greater unity in Western Europe, not to close and bolt the doors to future association of one kind or another with the nations of Eastern Europe. All the various institutions, from OECD and the Council of Europe to the tighter community of the Six, should keep a flexibility to deal in a practical way with the East European states now and to forge institutional links with them in the future. It would be a grave mistake to put them out of mind or deliberately consign them to the Soviet bloc and consider their future as a matter to be settled only with Moscow.

Second, the Western nations should cultivate all kinds of economic, cultural, and other ties with Eastern Europe. Most of them are already doing so, though in a haphazard and uncoordinated way, especially in respect of trade policy. We should not deceive ourselves regarding the unrepresentative character of the East European regimes, but there is little question that increased contact with them and with their peoples is more likely to encourage trends favorable to the latter than is a policy of boycott and isolation. Good results are more evident when the initiatives are carefully prepared and the process is selective, but in the exchange of persons, goods and ideas, mere volume can have its

[7] On this subject the arguments of Zbigniew Brzezinski, *Alternative to Partition* (New York: McGraw-Hill, for the Council on Foreign Relations, 1965) are of particular interest.

effect. Tourism in today's Europe can be a greater revolutionary force than Marxism. All these considerations may apply to Russia as well, but are much more promising in relation to the smaller states of Eastern Europe with their historic ties to the West.

Third, efforts at détente and settlement through negotiation with the Soviet Union and the East European states should not cease. Disengagement, arms control, European security—all the perennial topics of East-West debate—should be discussed and discussed again, with a hard-headed concern for the interests of the West and of the East European peoples. A real European settlement, ending the cold war and the partition of Germany and of Europe, may not be possible until some distant day, but progress on these related problems, which take on different colors and dimensions with the passage of time, could make that day come sooner.

In all these matters Yugoslavia may have an important role. Looking ahead, the big question is not how Yugoslavia can be drawn closer to the Western community—though that is important—but how Yugoslavia can help in bringing order and unity to Europe, in ending the cold war on acceptable terms. Yugoslavia already has close relations with some Western European nations and with the growing European institutions. It has already experienced broad economic and cultural contacts with the West. It has already settled, in friendly negotiations with Western countries, some of its most prickly international disputes: the Trieste settlement with Italy was a model in that it not only removed the inflammation on the borders of the two states but opened the way for a remarkably cordial relationship between them. As a small nation in a border area of Europe long contested between great powers, Yugoslavia cannot stand on its own. Its ties with the third world offer no salvation. It has to be in the East and in the West. Its interests force it to work for Europe.

Geography should not be ignored in any estimate of Yugoslavia's role in the making of a new Europe. Because of the unique position it has gained in world politics and because the horizons of its leaders have stretched far beyond Europe, it is sometimes forgotten that this "heroic age" may not last forever. The importance of Yugoslavia for the future of Europe has already been mentioned. As events work out, its main role may well be in its own area of the Danube basin and the Balkans.

To the north, where Yugoslavia is not physically present, the problems of German unification and of Polish-German settlement may be intractable for a long time. They involve such major security interests of the great powers that Yugoslavia is not likely to exert a great influence one way or the other. In southeastern Europe, on the other hand, Yugoslavia is very much present, and there the Soviet Union's security interests are not so strong, as shown by its original decision against invading Yugoslavia in 1948, its acceptance of Albania's defection, and its caution in dealing with Rumania. Tito's "Balkan imperialism" of 1947 and 1948, which so aroused Stalin's suspicion when there were plans for federation with Bulgaria and Albania and talk of a wider grouping, has not been forgotten in Yugoslavia, in neighboring states, or in Moscow. But the situation is now different. Yugoslavia cannot build a Communist empire and does not wish to; it looks toward closer relations with non-Communist Greece and Turkey as well as with Communist neighbors, largely ignoring the differences of political systems and of international alignment. Yugoslavia and Rumania are the two largest states in the Balkans and the most independent of all the Communist states of Eastern Europe; together they could exert a strong influence. There is no hint of a regional organization or alliance, but that is not the point. The point is that this area of Europe, with Yugoslavia in a key position, could develop regional interests which are not Soviet interests, new relationships which gradually and effectively could end Soviet domination of any part of it, and do so without the intervention of American power, the intensification of the cold war, or any revolutionary change in the official ideologies or political systems of the states involved.

The purpose of these rather speculative comments is to illustrate what may happen when the rigid patterns of the cold-war period begin to break up. In a situation where American policy in Europe must go beyond mere organization for defense and advocacy of Western unity, the task ahead is to find measures of broader scope which move matters more actively toward the twin goals of reunification of Germany and the drawing together of

Eastern and Western Europe, whether by agreement with the Soviet Union or by encouraging trends which the Soviet Union will have to accept. An American policy which does not take account of Yugoslavia's special situation and its potential influence will suffer serious and unnecessary handicaps.

Yugoslavia's role over the longer term goes beyond its politics of last year or of next year. Even the question of its Communist regime may not be with us indefinitely. Who can say where the "road to socialism" will have led ten years from now? The country may become absorbed in its own internal crises, a Balkan backwater; or it may become a stage where the great forces of our time meet in contention or in reconciliation, with consequences extending far beyond Yugoslavia's borders.

The larger perspective brings us back to two themes of the opening chapter. The greatest problem for the Yugoslavs is the conflict of their own different nationalities; if they can control and eventually solve it, there can be little question that they will have a constructive role to play in Europe. Finally, the popular forces in the country, which the regime cannot suppress but seems rather to absorb and to change itself in so doing, see their ultimate interests and those of that part of Europe as in harmony with the Western world.

# APPENDIX TABLE

U.S. FOREIGN ASSISTANCE TO YUGOSLAVIA

Obligations and Loan Authorizations
(in millions of dollars)

| Fiscal Year | Loans | Grants | Public Law 480 | | |
| --- | --- | --- | --- | --- | --- |
| | | | Title I Sales for Dinars | Titles II and III Emergency Relief and Grants to Voluntary Relief Agencies | Title IV Dollar Credit Sales |
| 1950 | 40.0 | — | | | |
| 1951 | 15.0 | 92.9* | | | |
| 1952 | — | 81.5 | | 24.8† | |
| 1953 | — | 122.4 | | 0.2† | — |
| 1954 | — | 66.5 | | 1.1† | — |
| 1955 | — | 42.7 | 49.5 | 61.9 | — |
| Total | 136.5 | 27.2 | 356.0 | 112.4 | — |
| 1956 | 15.0 | 14.8 | 70.8 | 8.7 | — |
| 1957 | 13.5 | 1.3 | 99.3 | 32.8 | — |
| 1958 | 8.0 | 3.4 | 71.9 | 28.8 | — |
| 1959 | 59.2 | 3.9 | 94.8 | 27.9 | — |
| 1960 | 40.8 | 3.8 | 19.2 | 14.2 | — |
| Total | 136.5 | 27.2 | 356.0 | 112.4 | — |
| 1961 | 102.7 | 3.3 | 30.4 | 14.1 | — |
| 1962 | — | 0.5 | 93.1 | 15.1 | 17.3 |
| 1963 | −0.8 | −0.2 | 92.1 | 14.3 | 16.2 |
| 1964 | — | −0.4 | 18.2 | 13.4 | 46.1 |
| 1965 | −0.3 | −0.1 | — | 3.6 | 94.1 |
| Total | 101.6 | 3.1 | 233.8 | 60.5 | 173.7 |
| Grand Total | 293.1 | 436.3 | 639.3 | 260.9 | 173.7 |

NOTES: * Includes $50 million under Yugoslav Emergency Relief Act of 1950 (using funds appropriated for ECA)
† Extended under Agricultural Act of 1949 (prior to PL 480). The 1952 total covers fiscal years 1950–52.

SOURCES: Adapted from Agency for International Development, *U.S. Foreign Assistance and Assistance from International Organizations*, July 1, 1945–June 30, 1961, p. 25; Same, July 1. 1945–June 30, 1962, p. 126; Same, Special Report prepared for the House Foreign Affairs Committee, *U.S. Overseas Loans and Grants and Assistance from International Organizations*, July 1, 1945–June 30, 1965, p. 137.

# Index

## PUBLICATIONS

FOREIGN AFFAIRS (quarterly), edited by Hamilton Fish Armstrong.

THE UNITED STATES IN WORLD AFFAIRS (annual). Volumes for 1931, 1932 and 1933, by Walter Lippmann and William O. Scroggs; for 1934-1935, 1936, 1937, 1938, 1939 and 1940, by Whitney H. Shepardson and William O. Scroggs; for 1945-1947, 1947-1948 and 1948-1949, by John C. Campbell; for 1949, 1950, 1951, 1952, 1953 and 1954, by Richard P. Stebbins; for 1955, by Hollis W. Barber; for 1956, 1957, 1958, 1959, 1960, 1961, 1962 and 1963, by Richard P. Stebbins; for 1964, by Jules Davids; for 1965, by Richard P. Stebbins.

DOCUMENTS ON AMERICAN FOREIGN RELATIONS (annual). Volume for 1952 edited by Clarence W. Baier and Richard P. Stebbins; for 1953 and 1954, edited by Peter V. Curl; for 1955, 1956, 1957, 1958 and 1959, edited by Paul E. Zinner; for 1960, 1961, 1962 and 1963, edited by Richard P. Stebbins; for 1964, edited by Jules

Davids; for 1965, edited by Richard P. Stebbins.

POLITICAL HANDBOOK AND ATLAS OF THE WORLD (annual), edited by Walter H. Mallory.

U.S. TRADE POLICY: New Legislation for the Next Round, by John W. Evans (1967).

THE ARTILLERY OF THE PRESS: Its Influence on American Foreign Policy, by James Reston (1967).

ATLANTIC ECONOMIC COOPERATION: The Case of the OECD, by Henry Aubrey (1967).

TRADE, AID AND DEVELOPMENT: The Rich and Poor Nations, by John Pincus (1967).

BETWEEN TWO WORLDS: Policy, Press and Public Opinion on Asian-American Relations, by John Hohenberg (1967).

THE CONFLICTED RELATIONSHIP: The West and the Transformation of Asia, Africa and Latin America, by Theodore Geiger (1967).

THE ATLANTIC IDEA AND ITS EUROPEAN RIVALS, by H. van B. Cleveland (1966).

EUROPEAN UNIFICATION IN THE SIXTIES: From the Veto to the Crisis, by Miriam Camps (1966).

THE UNITED STATES AND CHINA IN WORLD AFFAIRS, by Robert Blum, edited by A. Doak Barnett (1966).

THE FUTURE OF THE OVERSEAS CHINESE IN SOUTHEAST ASIA, by Lea A. Williams (1966).

THE CONSCIENCE OF THE RICH NATIONS: The Development Assistance Committee and the Common Aid Effort, by Seymour J. Rubin (1966).

ATLANTIC AGRICULTURAL UNITY: Is It Possible?, by John O. Coppock (1966).

COMMUNIST CHINA'S ECONOMIC GROWTH AND FOREIGN TRADE, by Alexander Eckstein (1966).

TEST BAN AND DISARMAMENT: THE PATH OF NEGOTIATION, by Arthur H. Dean (1966).

THE AMERICAN PEOPLE AND CHINA, by A. T. Steele (1966).

POLICIES TOWARD CHINA: VIEWS FROM SIX CONTINENTS, edited by A. M. Halpern (1966).

INTERNATIONAL POLITICAL COMMUNICATION, by W. Phillips Davison (1965).

MONETARY REFORM FOR THE WORLD ECONOMY, by Robert V. Roosa (1965).

AFRICAN BATTLELINE: American Policy Choices in Southern Africa, by Waldemar A. Nielsen (1965).

NATO IN TRANSITION: The Future of the Atlantic Alliance, by Timothy W. Stanley (1965).

ALTERNATIVE TO PARTITION: For a Broader Conception of America's Role in Europe, by Zbigniew Brzezinski (1965).

THE TROUBLED PARTNERSHIP: A Re-Appraisal of the Atlantic Alliance, by Henry A. Kissinger (1965).

REMNANTS OF EMPIRE: The United Nations and the End of Colonialism, by David W. Wainhouse (1965).

THE EUROPEAN COMMUNITY AND AMERICAN TRADE: A Study in Atlantic Economics and Policy, by Randall Hinshaw (1964).

THE FOURTH DIMENSION OF FOREIGN POLICY: Educational and Cultural Affairs, by Philip H. Coombs (1964).

AMERICAN AGENCIES INTERESTED IN INTERNATIONAL AFFAIRS (Fifth Edition), compiled by Donald Wasson (1964).

JAPAN AND THE UNITED STATES IN WORLD TRADE, by Warren S. Hunsberger (1964).

FOREIGN AFFAIRS BIBLIOGRAPHY, 1952-1962, by Henry L. Roberts (1964).

THE DOLLAR IN WORLD AFFAIRS: An Essay in International Financial Policy, by Henry G. Aubrey (1964).

ON DEALING WITH THE COMMUNIST WORLD, by George F. Kennan (1964).

FOREIGN AID AND FOREIGN POLICY, by Edward S. Mason (1964).

THE SCIENTIFIC REVOLUTION AND WORLD POLITICS, by Caryl P. Haskins (1964).

AFRICA: A Foreign Affairs Reader, edited by Philip W. Quigg (1964).

THE PHILIPPINES AND THE UNITED STATES: Problems of Partnership, by George E. Taylor (1964).

SOUTHEAST ASIA IN UNITED STATES POLICY, by Russell H. Fifield (1963).

UNESCO: ASSESSMENT AND PROMISE, by George N. Shuster (1963).

THE PEACEFUL ATOM IN FOREIGN POLICY, by Arnold Kramish (1963).

THE ARABS AND THE WORLD: Nasser's Arab Nationalist Policy, by Charles D. Cremeans (1963).

TOWARD AN ATLANTIC COMMUNITY, by Christian A. Herter (1963).

THE SOVIET UNION, 1922-1962: A Foreign Affairs Reader, edited by Philip E. Mosely (1963).

THE POLITICS OF FOREIGN AID: American Experience in Southeast Asia, by John D. Montgomery (1962).

SPEARHEADS OF DEMOCRACY: Labor in the Developing Countries, by George C. Lodge (1962).

LATIN AMERICA: Diplomacy and Reality, by Adolf A. Berle (1962).

THE ORGANIZATION OF AMERICAN STATES AND THE HEMISPHERE CRISIS, by John C. Dreier (1962).

THE UNITED NATIONS: Structure for Peace, by Ernest A. Gross (1962).

THE LONG POLAR WATCH: Canada and the Defense of North America, by Melvin Conant (1962).

ARMS AND POLITICS IN LATIN AMERICA (Revised Edition), by Edwin Lieuwen (1961).

THE FUTURE OF UNDERDEVELOPED COUNTRIES: Political Implications of Economic Development (Revised Edition), by Eugene Staley (1961).

SPAIN AND DEFENSE OF THE WEST: Ally and Liability, by Arthur P. Whitaker (1961).

SOCIAL CHANGE IN LATIN AMERICA TODAY: Its Implications for United States Policy, by Richard N. Adams, John P. Gillin, Allan R. Holmberg, Oscar Lewis, Richard W. Patch, and Charles W. Wagley (1961).

FOREIGN POLICY: THE NEXT PHASE: The 1960s (Revised Edition), by Thomas K. Finletter (1960).

DEFENSE OF THE MIDDLE EAST: Problems of American Policy (Revised Edition), by John C. Campbell (1960).

COMMUNIST CHINA AND ASIA: Challenge to American Policy, by A. Doak Barnett (1960).

FRANCE, TROUBLED ALLY: De Gaulle's Heritage and Prospects, by Edgar S. Furniss, Jr. (1960).